Automating ActionScript Projects with Eclipse and Ant

Sidney de Koning

O'REILLY®

Beijing · Cambridge · Farnham · Köln · Sebastopol · Tokyo

Automating ActionScript Projects with Eclipse and Ant

by Sidney de Koning

Published by O'Reilly Media, Inc., 1005 Gravenstein Highway North, Sebastopol, CA 95472.

O'Reilly books may be purchased for educational, business, or sales promotional use. Online editions are also available for most titles (*http://my.safaribooksonline.com*). For more information, contact our corporate/institutional sales department: (800) 998-9938 or *corporate@oreilly.com*.

Editor:	Mary Treseler	**Cover Designer:**	Karen Montgomery
Production Editor:	Teresa Elsey	**Interior Designer:**	David Futato
Copyeditor:	Rachel Monaghan	**Illustrator:**	Robert Romano
Technical Editor:	Patrick Rushton		

Revision History for the First Edition:

2011-10-07   First release

See *http://oreilly.com/catalog/errata.csp?isbn=9781449307738* for release details.

ISBN: 978-1-449-30773-8

[LSI]

1318000991

Adobe Developer Library

Adobe Developer Library, a copublishing partnership between O'Reilly Media Inc., and Adobe Systems, Inc., is the authoritative resource for developers using Adobe technologies. These comprehensive resources offer learning solutions to help developers create cutting-edge interactive web applications that can reach virtually anyone on any platform.

With top quality books and innovative online resources covering the latest tools for rich-Internet application development, the *Adobe Developer Library* delivers expert training straight from the source. Topics include ActionScript, Adobe Flex®, Adobe Flash®, and Adobe Acrobat®.

Get the latest news about books, online resources, and more at *http://adobedeveloper library.com*.

Table of Contents

Preface

Introduction

Let me start by saying I'm a lazy developer by design. I'd rather spend a day to code something once than code the same task over and over again. The same goes for processes: why do repetitive tasks if you can automate them? Imagine all the time you'll save. We live in a world where time is scarce and where project managers are breathing down our necks to get that specific feature, that deployment, or that project done *now*.

Just think of all the stress it will save you when you return to that project you did a year ago and you can just build with the push of a button. Less stress, *and* more control over your workflow.

And besides that, computers were designed to do only one task for you: compute (and, if programmed correctly, help you solve problems).

That is what this book is about: giving you the tools and knowledge to set up your own "ultimate development machine" to help you code, compile, debug, and deploy faster—i.e., to automate the whole process that takes place beyond the initial programming.

Build Systems

Before I started this book, I did a survey to see if people were using build systems as part of their daily workflow. Almost 50 people participated—not many, but it gave me a fairly accurate picture. My results showed that 95 percent of the people who filled in the survey were aware that they could automate their workflows for ActionScript development. But only 66 percent use build systems in their daily workflow.

The most common reasons people gave for not using build systems were: "Too difficult," "Our projects are not large enough," "Perfectly happy doing it my way," and "It takes more time, but I'm fine with that."

Well, I'm here to prove otherwise. I'll show you that it is not hard to make a consistent workflow for multiple machines, even complete departments. I'll show you that with minimum effort, you can have Ant do all the hard work for you.

It doesn't matter if you are doing a big or small project; all projects benefit from automation. They all need to be done under a high-pressure deadline, and Ant can help you with that. The only thing you need is a little time.

Most of the people who participated in my survey (but also in the Flash community at large) use either FlashBuilder or FDT, and since both are based on Eclipse, this book focuses on this IDE.

What do I hope to accomplish with this book? A small revolution, where every Flash developer knows what build systems are and can use them to his advantage—and on a daily basis. Because build systems are sexy! And they make your life so much easier! So you can spend time on the stuff that matters most, creating the stuff you love.

Audience

This book is mainly written for:

- Flash developers who want to step up their workflow
- The junior Flash developer who wants to take his game to a new level and work smarter, not faster
- The senior who has been doing the same trick for many years
- People who want to spend their time more effectively, so they don't have to work late and can have time left for thinking about the stuff that's important to them and building things they love, like their own framework, libraries, or tools
- And, of course, every developer in between

Contents of This Book

This book is divided into three chapters.

In Chapter 1, *Tools*, I'll guide you through the installation and setup of your workspace and discuss the Eclipse plug-in FDT, issue- and bug-tracking integration in Eclipse with Mylyn, the Android SDK, and everything else you need to get started.

Chapter 2, *Source Code Management*, defines source code management, including a discussion of SVN and Git and their basic commands, and describes how you can use it for your benefit.

In Chapter 3, *Automation*, I'll talk about what Apache Ant is and why it is so powerful, how you can integrate it with FDT, and how Ant can take away a lot of manual work. I'll also give you loads of code examples to help you build, compile, deploy, and otherwise manage your projects.

You can find all the source code for this book at *http://book.funky-monkey.nl/*.

Conventions Used in This Book

The following typographical conventions are used in this book:

Italic
> Indicates new terms, URLs, email addresses, filenames, file extensions, pathnames, directories, and Unix utilities.

`Constant width`
> Indicates commands, options, switches, variables, attributes, keys, functions, types, classes, namespaces, methods, modules, properties, parameters, values, objects, events, event handlers, XML tags, HTML tags, macros, the contents of files, or the output from commands.

`Constant width bold`
> Shows commands or other text that should be typed literally by the user.

`Constant width italic`
> Shows text that should be replaced with user-supplied values.

 This icon signifies a tip, suggestion, or general note.

 This icon indicates a warning or caution.

Using Code Examples

This book is here to help you get your job done. In general, you may use the code in this book in your programs and documentation. You do not need to contact us for permission unless you're reproducing a significant portion of the code. For example, writing a program that uses several chunks of code from this book does not require permission. Selling or distributing a CD-ROM of examples from O'Reilly books does require permission. Answering a question by citing this book and quoting example code does not require permission. Incorporating a significant amount of example code from this book into your product's documentation does require permission.

We appreciate, but do not require, attribution. An attribution usually includes the title, author, publisher, and ISBN. For example: "*Automating ActionScript Projects with Eclipse and Ant* by Sidney de Koning (O'Reilly). Copyright 2012 Sidney de Koning, 978-1-449-30773-8."

If you feel your use of code examples falls outside fair use or the permission given above, feel free to contact us at *permissions@oreilly.com*.

We'd Like to Hear from You

Please address comments and questions concerning this book to the publisher:

O'Reilly Media, Inc.
1005 Gravenstein Highway North
Sebastopol, CA 95472
(800) 998-9938 (in the United States or Canada)
(707) 829-0515 (international or local)
(707) 829-0104 (fax)

We have a web page for this book, where we list errata, examples, and any additional information. You can access this page at:

http://shop.oreilly.com/product/0636920020950.do

To comment or ask technical questions about this book, send email to:

bookquestions@oreilly.com

For more information about our books, courses, conferences, and news, see our website at *http://www.oreilly.com*.

Find us on Facebook: *http://facebook.com/oreilly*

Follow us on Twitter: *http://twitter.com/oreillymedia*

Watch us on YouTube: *http://www.youtube.com/oreillymedia*

Safari® Books Online

Safari Safari Books Online is an on-demand digital library that lets you easily search over 7,500 technology and creative reference books and videos to find the answers you need quickly.

With a subscription, you can read any page and watch any video from our library online. Read books on your cell phone and mobile devices. Access new titles before they are available for print, and get exclusive access to manuscripts in development and post feedback for the authors. Copy and paste code samples, organize your favorites, download chapters, bookmark key sections, create notes, print out pages, and benefit from tons of other time-saving features.

O'Reilly Media has uploaded this book to the Safari Books Online service. To have full digital access to this book and others on similar topics from O'Reilly and other publishers, sign up for free at *http://my.safaribooksonline.com*.

Acknowledgments

I'd like to acknowledge the following people, each of whom had something to do with the creation of this book.

Thank you to my girlfriend, Jess, for everything she had to endure these last months and for giving me the motivation when I needed it. And, yes, we will plan that vacation now! Thanks to all my mentors throughout my career, especially Donovan, who taught me how to focus on one thing only—those lessons paid off in the form of this book. Thank you to my mom, Tries, and her hubby, Sietso, for giving me the tools to accomplish anything. And to the rest: Robert de Koning, Patrick Rushton, and Alex Collins—you all rock!

And, of course, to the Flash community: this is me giving back for everything I've learned over the years. Hope you put it to good use and create amazing things with it.

## CHAPTER 1

Tools

In every construction project, the foundation is the most important part; without it, the whole building comes tumbling down. So, before we can do anything, we need to have the right tools to lay our foundation.

Although all the tools we will use are available on most platforms, I use Mac OS X throughout this book. For Windows users, the process is almost the same, although UI buttons and menus might be located elsewhere. I'm not biased in any way; an OS is a tool in your toolbox, and it should be treated as such.

If you already have Eclipse, FDT, and the Android SDK installed, you can skip to Chapter 2. However, even if you already know this material or have these tools installed, you'll likely find some valuable tips and lessons in this chapter. I highly recommend that you at least browse through it.

Eclipse

Since the examples in this book revolve around the Eclipse IDE, we will start by downloading it from the following location: *http://www.eclipse.org/downloads/*.

The current version of Eclipse at the time of this writing is Indigo.

You are presented with a number of choices; pick "Eclipse IDE for Java Developers." It is one of the smallest options in file size, and it already includes a CVS client, an XML editor, and the Mylyn plug-in. We will talk more about plug-ins later; for now, just unpack the downloaded package to run the Eclipse application.

Workspaces and Perspectives

When you open Eclipse after the splash screen, you are presented with a dialog window asking you to specify a location for your workspace. Normally, you would choose your user directory and then a folder called *workspace* (it defaults to the *Documents* directory within the user's home folder), but you can choose any location.

What are workspaces?

Workspaces are what make Eclipse so powerful. A workspace is a folder on your hard drive that holds all your settings, color themes, code formatting, and other preferences. It also keeps your projects organized. There are different ways you can organize; for example, a workspace can hold all your projects for a specific client but also for a specific language. As we noticed when downloading Eclipse, you could download different versions for specific languages (Java, C++, PHP, JavaScript, etc.). And since every development plug-in has a different *perspective*, we could easily edit XML in the XML perspective and then switch to the FDT perspective to edit our ActionScript class files—all in one workspace. (See Figure 1-1.)

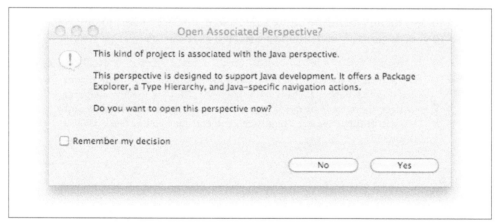

Figure 1-1. Opening different perspectives

Just think of perspectives as different glasses you use to see everything around you. One allows you to see everything XML-related; another, everything JavaScript-related. But you can take this concept one level further by leveraging the power of workspaces.

My workspaces are set up in such a way that I have one for normal ActionScript projects, one for "AIR for Android" development, one for AIR development, and so on.

You can also set up workspaces in such a way that you have one workspace for your work projects, one for your personal pet projects, and one for creating *POC (proof of concepts)* or prototypes. Or you might even have one workspace per client. It all depends on what you like and how organized you are.

Another good reason to set up multiple workspaces is if you use different languages; you can set up one language per space, and it will be used on all your projects in that workspace. This is a one-time process, and you can edit the preferences after you have created a new workspace.

Once you have chosen where to put the workspace, there are a couple of settings we want to change globally in Eclipse—just some little things that'll make your life easier.

Preferences

Open up the Preference panel by going to Eclipse→Preferences→General. Now check the "Show heap status" option (Figure 1-2). This displays an icon at the bottom right of the main Eclipse window indicating the amount of memory used by every operation that Eclipse performs. The bin icon next to it enables you to purge or kick-start the garbage collection to free memory.

Figure 1-2. Show heap status

Increase Eclipse's Available Memory

The next thing we need to do to make Eclipse a lean and mean machine is to set the available memory higher. These memory settings are in a file called *eclipse.ini*. On Windows, just search for that file in the install directory where Eclipse resides. On a Mac, it works a little differently. Right-click the *Eclipse.app* file and select Show Package Contents. Now browse to the *Contents/MacOS* folder. Open up *Eclipse.ini* in your favorite text editor and look for the values -Xms and -Xmx.

The default values for Eclipse are -Xms40m and -Xmx384m. I've found they work best if you set -Xms to 512m and -Xmx to 1024m. This should give you enough available memory to work with. Just make sure when editing this file to keep each argument on a single line; if you put more on one line, the JVM (Java Virtual Machine) will ignore them:

```
-vmargs
-Dosgi.requiredJavaVersion=1.5
-XstartOnFirstThread
-Dorg.eclipse.swt.internal.carbon.smallFonts
-XX:MaxPermSize=256m
-Xms512m
-Xmx1024m
-Xdock:icon=../Resources/Eclipse.icns
-XstartOnFirstThread
```

Shortcut Keys

Most people are used to working with the Flash IDE, so it makes sense to set the shortcut key for compiling to Command-Enter (Ctrl-Enter on Windows). Open up the Eclipse preference pane and in the search box, type **key**. This brings up a selection of possible items you are searching for.

The option we are looking for is under General→Keys; here, you'll find the key bindings (Figure 1-3). Now search for Run Last Launched, and change the binding to Command-Enter (Ctrl-Enter on Windows). You do this by simply pressing those keys in the binding field. And since we want this to always happen when we're compiling/debugging, we also need to set another option.

Go back to the main search field in the Eclipse preferences and type **config**. This should bring up the Run/Debug→Launching options. At the bottom, you will find the "Always launch the previously launched application" option that you need to select (Figure 1-4). Click Apply and OK to confirm, and we are all set (for now).

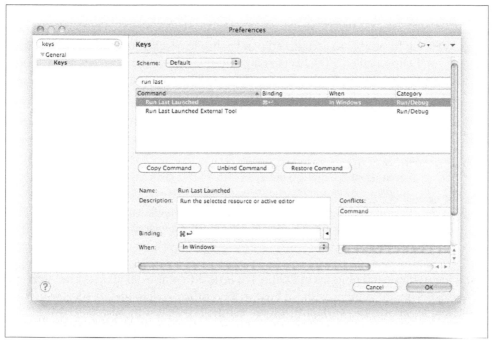

Figure 1-3. Setting the key bindings

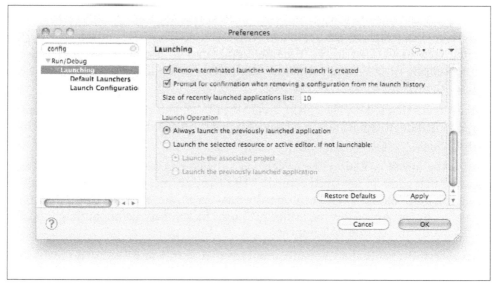

Figure 1-4. Always launch the previously launched application

FDT

Next, we want to be able to actually edit and compile AS class files. We do this with a plug-in for Eclipse called FDT. Personally, I think this is the best editor for doing ActionScript work, but as I said, this is personal. There are tons of editors out there, but for this book we will be using FDT.

One of the cool things about FDT is that if you create open source projects, you can apply for a free FDT Max license.

 For more information on the features that FDT offers, go to *http://www .fdt.powerflasher.com/developer-tools/fdt/features/*.

For more information about FDT's open source initiative and free FDT Max license, go to *http://www.fdt.powerflasher.com/developer-tools/fdt/ community/*.

Installing updates and plug-ins in Eclipse is a little different from all the other software downloads you are familiar with. Eclipse works with so-called *update sites*, which are basically file repositories with an XML file defining the latest builds.

So, instead of going to a download site and downloading a package, we open the Help panel and select the Install New Software option. (See Figure 1-5.)

Enter the URL to the update site from FDT: *http://fdt.powerflasher.com/update*.

After you click Add, you are presented with a couple of choices; at the time of this writing, they are FDT 3.5 and FDT 4.4. Select the latest version and click Next to install it into Eclipse. After Eclipse calculates which elements to download and install, you will see the screen shown in Figure 1-6.

In the screens that follow, click Next, accept the EULA, and click Finish. Now it's time to get something to drink and stretch your legs a bit, because this part can take a while, depending on your connection speed.

During the install procedure, you might get a dialog box saying, "You are installing software that contains unsigned content." This basically means that there are plug-ins being installed that have not been signed with a certificate. In some cases, this could be malicious software. However, since FDT tests its software before putting it on the market, you can press the OK button.

After everything is installed, you are prompted to restart; you'll need to do so to complete the install process.

Congratulations! We have installed Eclipse and FDT. Now go the FDT website to get your trial license and get started: *http://www.fdt.powerflasher.com/getlicense*.

Thankfully, Ant is also installed with Eclipse, so we don't have to do anything additional for it. The Ant version at the time of this writing is 1.8.2.

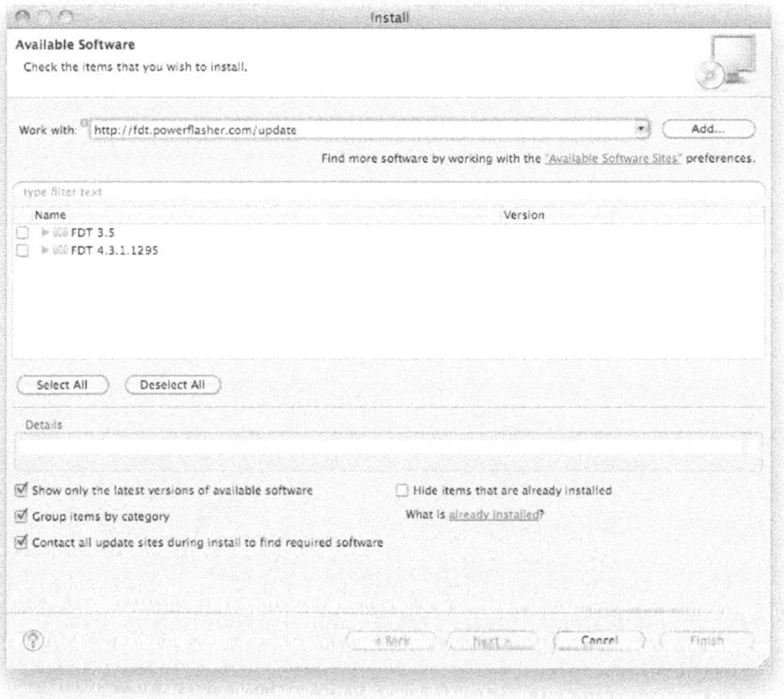

Figure 1-5. Updating software in Eclipse

Downloading the Android SDK

Go to *http://developer.android.com/sdk/index.html* and download the latest version. At the time of this writing, the latest version is R12, or release 12. Installing an SDK is easy: just download and extract the files. I place mine in the root of my hard drive in a folder called *SDK* and differentiate the files by version number. When you extract the Android SDK it should give you a folder with a name similar to *SDK/android-sdk-r12-mac_x86*.

Installing the ADT Plug-in for Eclipse

For Eclipse to work with Android, we have to install a new plug-in. Go to Help→Install New Software, and then click the big Add button on the right side of this screen. Here, you need to type in the URL of the ADT install site as follows: *https://dl-ssl.google.com/android/eclipse/*. For the name, you can enter **ADT Android** and click OK. This will search for the install site; when it is found, select all the options under Developer Tools, click Next, and then click Next again on the review screen. Accept the terms and click Finish. This should install everything you need. You might see a pop up saying you are

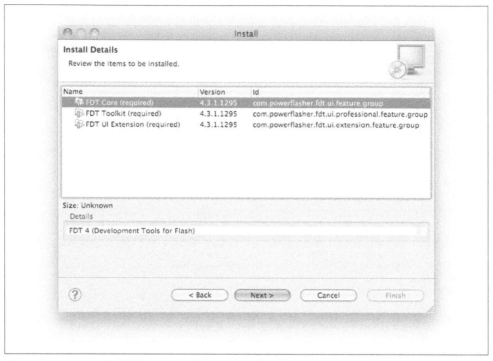

Figure 1-6. Review the FDT plug-in before it is installed

about to install unsigned content; this is the same pop up I mentioned during the FDT installation. You can click OK here. If everything is installed successfully, you will be presented with one final dialog. Just click the Restart Now button.

The last step of the Android ADT installation is to point to the Android SDK we downloaded earlier. Open up Eclipse's preferences and click the Android section. Here, you can fill in the path to your copy of the Android SDK.

Installing Android SDK Platform Tools

To use the Emulator, we need to first install the SDK platform tools. To do this, go to Window→"Android SDK and AVD Manager" (Figure 1-7).

When you select the "Available packages" option on the left, you can open the Android Repository and select everything from API level 8 through API level 13. You only have to do this for the SDKs. Since we are not doing any actual Android development and just need certain assets from this installation, we can leave the installation of these examples for now (of course, this is entirely up to you). In the following dialog, select Accept All to begin the installation.

Installing all these items will take a long time, so make yourself a cup of tea or coffee.

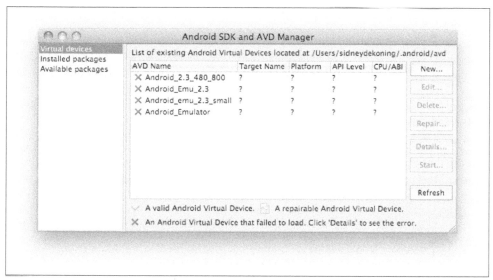

Figure 1-7. The Android Virtual Device Manager

After the installation has finished, you can close the screen and go back to "Installed packages" on the left. If everything went according to plan, you should see a bunch of installed items here.

If you go back to "Virtual devices," you should now see a premade 2.2 Emulator ready to use.

> You can also create your own emulator that targets a different version. AIR 2.7 supports the 2.2, 2.3, and 3.0 versions of the Android SDK.

Next, we'll configure Mylyn.

Mylyn

Mylyn is a plug-in for Eclipse that manages your bugs, issues, and tasks, but it can also be used for online project management. How does this work? Mylyn connects to your favorite bug- or issue-tracking system and reads all these issues per project, specified with *queries* (which we'll cover in more detail in "Adding a Repository to Mylyn" on page 12). It then generates a list for you to work on. You can even track your time working on that specific issue or bug.

A *bug-* or *issue-tracking system* allows you to keep track of all of the faults, issues, missing content, or misbehavior in a piece of software, without having to write them down. With an issue or bug tracker, you have one centralized place where you can manage, prioritize, or assign bugs and issues to different people so they can work on resolving them.

The big benefit of using Mylyn is that it enables you to do all of the above directly from within Eclipse.

By default, Mylyn has connectors for Bugzilla, JIRA, Mantis, Foglyn, and Trac, so if you are using one of those systems, you are in luck. (If not, you can look through the Eclipse Marketplace to see if there is a connector for your favorite bug tracker.)

A good option, especially if you are writing software for the community, is Mantis. It's free and open source, and you can run it on your own server. It only requires PHP and MySQL to be installed. For installation and more information, see *http://www.mantisbt.org/*.

Another option is Bugzilla, which is also free and open source and can be run on your own server. Unlike Mantis, however, Bugzilla requires you to run Perl on your server. Both Mozilla and Eclipse use Bugzilla to track their issues and bugs. More information is available at *http://www.bugzilla.org*.

Installing Connectors

To enable Mylyn to communicate with Google Code or GitHub, we need to install the appropriate plug-ins. (The process for the aforementioned connectors is practically the same, or even simpler.)

Google Code connector

We want to be able to view, edit, and resolve issues and tasks directly from Google Code in Eclipse so we can add comments, track our time spent on an issue, and change the status.

The first plug-in we will download is for Google Code. Remember, to install plug-ins or other packages in Eclipse, we go to Help→"Install new software." This presents us with a dialog box where we can input the download URL to the plug-in.

For more information on the Google Code Mylyn plug-in, see *http://code.google.com/p/googlecode-mylyn-connector/*.

At the time of this writing, this project is still actively being developed.

The install site for this plug-in is *http://knittig.de/googlecode-mylyn-connector/update/*.

Sometimes it is not possible to use the copy-and-paste keyboard short-cuts for URLs, passwords, or email addresses to Eclipse when you're working with the updater. The workaround is to use the right-click menu in the field you want to copy to and select Paste.

Select Nightly Builds and then the most current version. Then, simply go through all the install steps for this plug-in, accept the license agreement, and restart Eclipse.

Once you have restarted Eclipse, open a new perspective under Window→Open Perspective→Other. Now select Team Synchronizing. This opens the Task views as well. If you don't see them, you can open them by opening a view under Window→Show View→Task Lists or Task Repositories. For now, we are interested in the latter.

GitHub connector

If you would prefer to use GitHub instead of Google Code to host your open source projects, we need to integrate Git with Eclipse. We want to create our repository but also manage our open tasks.

If you are unfamiliar with Git and GitHub, don't worry—I will talk about them in more depth in Chapter 2. For now, we will just install the necessary plug-ins. If you want to jump ahead, you can learn about Git and GitHub in this introduction and video: *http://learn.github.com/p/intro.html*.

For now, we only want the EGit plug-in to be able to talk with our GitHub repository and get our tasks. (We will discuss the actual management of our repository in the following chapter.)

Installing this plug-in is a little different from contacting an install site, because we will make use of the Eclipse Marketplace. You can find this option under the Help menu.

Once we access the Marketplace, we can search for EGit. The installation process is relatively painless—just a matter of clicking Next and accepting the license agreement. Be sure to restart Eclipse if it asks you to do so.

If it doesn't work out for you with the Marketplace, you can try the update site by pasting this URL in the "Install new software" dialog box: *http://download.eclipse.org/releases/indigo/*.

In the Filter field, search for EGit. This should give you two options: Eclipse EGit and EGit Mylyn. Install both. I will save the explanation and actual use of EGit for Chapter 2.

Adding a Repository to Mylyn

Now that we have our favorite connector installed, we need to set up Mylyn. For Mylyn to work for us, we need to add a repository so we can get our tasks. If you don't have it open already, open the Tasks View by going to Window→Show View→Other→Mylyn. In the search box, type **mylyn**. You are now presented with only the Mylyn options.

Next, select the Add Task Repository icon in the Task Repository View. If everything went according to plan, you are now presented with a window that looks like Figure 1-8.

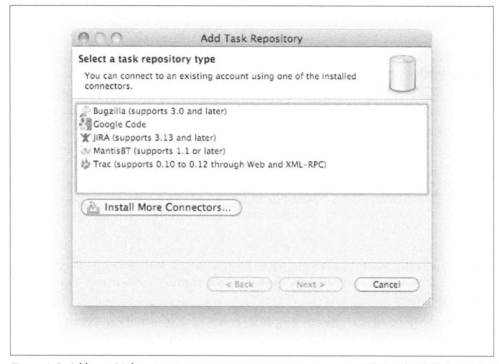

Figure 1-8. Adding a Mylyn repository

Here, we select the Google Code option and click Next, assuming you have an actual open source project hosted on Google Code. If you don't, you can create one; or, if you already know this process, you can skip ahead to the next chapter.

 Google Code offers free hosting for open source projects and comes with SVN, Git, or Mercurial access to your project. For more information about Google Code, go to *http://code.google.com/p/support/wiki/FAQ* and *http://code.google.com/hosting/createProject*.

Now you need to fill in the name of where the project is located—typically, that is something along the lines of *http://code.google.com/p/your_project_name/*—and your user credentials. (Make sure these are your Google Account credentials, *not* your Google Code password!)

The label field is just your own label to distinguish this task repository from the rest—something like My Project or Some AS3 API. When you click Finish, the task repository is created and you are asked if you would like to create a new query.

This step is basically a way for the connector to retrieve all the issues from Google Code. You can choose from predefined queries or create your own. For now, we will choose from the predefined; select Open Issues. After the synchronization process is done, you can double-click an issue in the Task List View and start working on it. You can always create more queries by right-clicking your repository and selecting New Query.

To get the hang of this task system, try creating an issue, editing its properties, and syncing it back to the repository.

The Task List should look something like Figure 1-9.

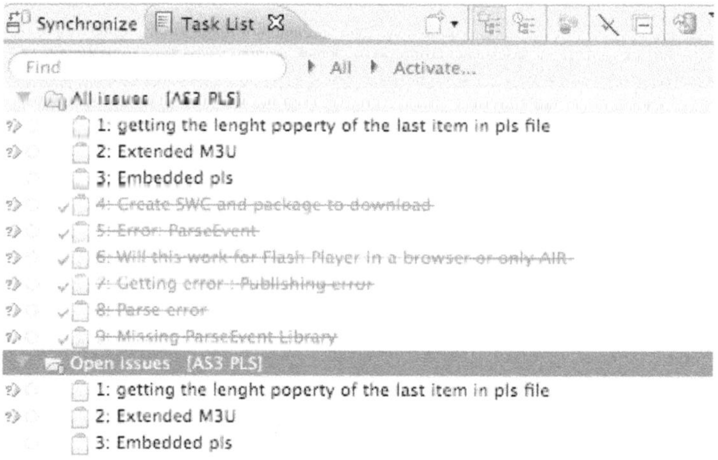

Figure 1-9. The Mylyn Task List

When you double-click an item in this list, Eclipse opens it in a special view. You can edit the issue, add comments about it, and change its priority. After you are done, submit it to make the changes permanent.

The process is pretty similar for other repositories. Try adding an issue with a different connector and see if you can add tasks and sync them back to the repository.

## CHAPTER 2

Source Code Management

Consider the following scenario. You have spent the past two days crafting the most perfect piece of code for your own library or framework. You ask your team member to create a practical example to test if it all works as you intended. You copy your source, and your teammate compiles it and finds a bug. Since he is a good team member, he wants to dive right into your code, fix it, and give you back the corrected code.

But after he fixes it, there are now two versions that need to be merged into one working piece of software. This can be a very error-prone and intimidating process: you have to identify what has changed and adjust it so it is correct in both versions.

Or what about this scenario? You are part of a team and need to work on the application for that Really Big Client. Since you work on location with the client and your colleague works back at your office, you can't work at the same time on the same code; you can only take turns with it. And since there is no centralized place to put the code, you have to copy over the source from your teammate before you can work on the project. Not very efficient!

This is where *source code management* (SCM) comes into play. SCM, or version control, is the practice of managing the revisions of your code with comments so the code can be easily retrieved, even if it was written a long time ago.

The best way to visualize a versioning system is to think of it as a tree. As a tree grows, layers develop, known as annual rings. With these rings, you can determine the tree's age. If you viewed a cross-section of the tree's trunk, you would see all the rings or yearly revisions. By examining the rings, you can see what the tree has gone through: rain or drought, good or bad nutrition, climate changes, amount of sun, and more. (This process is called dendrochronology, in case you are wondering.)

As with a tree, a versioning system also has a trunk and a branch or branches (and also something called a tag, but we'll get to that later). You can see what happened to your code in the past by looking at a specific revision. And the cool thing about a versioning system is that you can also go back in time and start from that point. You can't do that with a tree!

Another feature of a versioning system is the ability to merge code. Think of our previous scenarios. With a versioning system, you can work simultaneously with teammates now, and later in the project you can merge the code together and very easily resolve code conflicts.

Another good reason to have a centralized versioning system is what is called the "truck factor." What happens to your code if that one member of your team—the one who knows everything—is run over by a truck, with laptop and all? Can the team still work on the code, or is it all stored in the head and hard drive of that employee who's now lying in the hospital? Though that sounds very dramatic, all too often people forget to upload the assets (code, images, etc.) on which they're currently working to a server. When you're using a version control system, it can be as easy as pressing a single button.

There are a few features that a good versioning system must offer. For example, it must enable you to:

- Add, remove, rename, and delete files.
- See which files have been changed by which user and when.
- Keep track of different versions of the complete product (tags) and store them while working on the new version.
- Go back and forth between versions.
- Merge code (*merging*).
- Go back in time/undo (*reverting*).

Of course, as you can imagine, different versioning needs require different versioning tools. The two most commonly used tools at the moment are Subversion (SVN) and Git. There are other tools that provide almost or exactly the same functionality—e.g., Perforce, Mercurial, Bitkeeper, and CVS—but for now we will talk only about these two, because if you grasp the concepts behind them, the rest will be a breeze. Our discussion will also give you an overview of the tools' benefits and shortcomings. They all work a bit differently and were each created to target a specific problem.

SVN and Git

Let's start with SVN. Short for Subversion, SVN allows you to work with multiple people on a project. You create a new SVN project on a server, do a *checkout* (SVN's term for making a local copy) of files from the server, and *commit* (SVN's term for adding) the files to the server. During this process, SVN completely copies all the files to your local drive, and for every operation you will need a connection to the server.

Git works a bit differently. Unlike SVN, it doesn't copy the repository; rather, it clones it. This means that you have the complete repository running locally, and you can use it even without a connection to the Internet. So you can still perform actions like branching and merging (or any other action, for that matter) while working in a plane, bathroom, or any other WiFi-free zone. This is one of the strong advantages Git has over SVN.

 In British slang, a *git* is a person who is stupid or silly. The word is mostly used as an insult. Git got its name from its creator, Linus Torvalds, who explained, "I'm an egotistical bastard, and I name all my projects after myself. First Linux, now Git."

Some of the biggest differences between SVN and Git are:

- Git is *distributed*. This means no more sending email with software patches; just do a pull request.
- Git stores metadata instead of the actual files with every commit.
- Git can work without an active Internet connection; every operation you perform is local.
- SVN is based on WebDAV and stores complete files during commits.

Of course, there are many more differences, but they are beyond the scope of this book. For now, these are the most important to remember.

Now that we've covered what SVN and Git are, we need to talk about how you can use them to help you work faster and not stress over your code. Next, we will install SVN and Git clients for Eclipse and cover the basic steps for working with them.

SVN in Eclipse

Subversion in Eclipse can be handled via a plug-in called Subclipse. Just like when we installed FDT, we need to install Subclipse through an update site. Go to Help→Install Software and enter this address: *http://subclipse.tigris.org/update_1.6.x/*.

This will give you a bunch of options; check all of them and then click Next. You will probably be presented with a dialog box about unsigned software, but you can ignore this warning and proceed. After everything is installed, you'll be prompted to restart Eclipse.

If Eclipse is fully up and running, let's add a repository to our workspace. This assumes you are using a repository. If you're not, no problem; there are dozens of sites online that offer cheap or free SVN access where you can store your files. Open source developers can use Google Code or GitHub. However, most shops have their own SVN servers, either internally or externally hosted. If you don't, you should probably have a chat with someone at your shop about getting one. It is a crucial element for working with teams.

But for demonstration purposes, let's assume you have a server and we are going to connect to it. As an example, let's take an open source project: AS3 PLS Reader, a tool

I created to read playlist files from streaming radio servers and play them in Flash. The project URL is *http://code.google.com/p/as3plsreader/*, and the SVN checkout URL is *http://as3plsreader.googlecode.com/svn/*. You don't have write access to this project, but the operations we'll go over will give you a feel for how SVN works.

Open up Window→Views→Other. This will bring up a dialog with an SVN Repository Exploring option. Select it and click OK. This will open the SVN View. Since we want to add a repository, click the plus sign (+) in the top-right corner of this view (or right-click anywhere in this view and select New→"Repository location"). This brings up a dialog, shown in Figure 2-1, where you'll paste the URL of the repository in the URL field.

Figure 2-1. Adding an SVN repository

 If you get the error "Failed to load JavaHL," it means your operating system does not have the correct SVN libraries installed. Just go to this URL and install the package suitable for your OS: *http://www.open.col lab.net/downloads/community/*.

When you click Finish, the repository is added to the view and you will be able to make a checkout. If you open the newly created bookmark, you'll see the folders we already talked about: *trunk*, *branches*, and *tags* (and *wiki*, but that is specific to Google Code). Open up *trunk*, and you should see a bunch of files and folders. When you right-click on *trunk*, you can select "checkout." This brings up the screen shown in Figure 2-2.

We want to check out this project to our default Eclipse workspace, and we want it to be fully *recursive*—i.e., we want all the files, not just a subset. When you click Finish

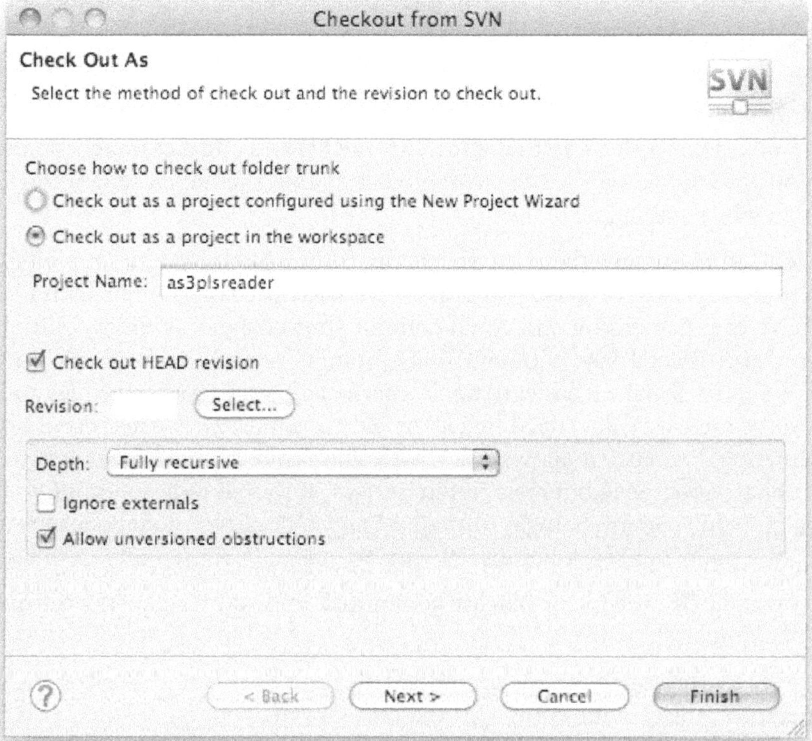

Figure 2-2. Doing a checkout from SVN

and go back to your FDT view, you'll see that SVN has created a project for us that is under version control.

If you look closely, you'll see icons and numbers next to the folders (Figure 2-3).

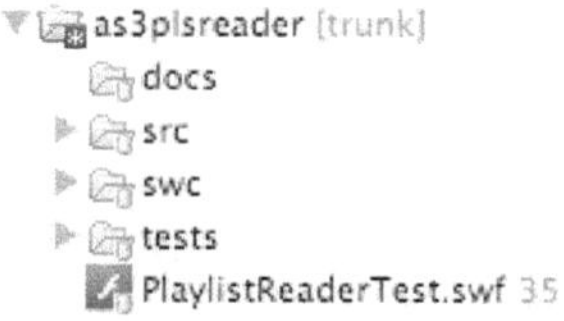

Figure 2-3. A checked-out project from SVN in your workspace

The numbers indicate the revision. Remember how we talked about the rings of a tree? This is the SVN equivalent.

For this project to become a Flash project that we can compile, we need to adjust the project's settings and add a Flash *nature* to it. Right-click on the folder labeled *[trunk]* and select Flash Project→Add Flash Nature; this lets us select the SDK we want to use for this project. Anything from Flex SDK 3.5 with AIR support will do.

Now, if we were to open a file and make changes to it, we would also want to save it back to SVN, right? So let's do that. Open up any file and add a comment somewhere. When you save it, you will see the icon indicating that the file has changed—a black box with a white star in it.

Next, we need to commit the changes back to SVN. (Although this step won't work for this sample project because you don't have write access, on your own SVN, you would have that permission and could commit your changes as follows.) Right-click on the file and select Team→Commit. This prompts us to provide a message for the commit, which will make it easier to track what exactly was done to the files and when. These can be messages like "fixed bug x" or "added some text." This is also known as the "blame log," because it allows you to see who broke or fixed the software. There is some debate about this, but my opinion is that you should only commit files that are not broken. Don't commit halfway through a bug fix, because if your colleague updates his SVN, his build will break because of you. So, *only commit fully functional source*.

When you click OK, the file or files are committed, and you have just performed your first SVN command!

If somebody else on your team has committed files and you want to work on the project, you'll need to replace your copy with the current one from SVN—i.e., you need to perform an update. This is essentially the same process as committing. Right-click on the project and select Team→"Update to HEAD." The HEAD is always the latest update, or latest revision.

Under the Team option, you will find all of the SVN commands you need. Just play around here and see what each does. Please note that it is better to experiment with the SVN command on your own project than in a production environment, because you can potentially break stuff—so, be careful.

Git in Eclipse

Git in Eclipse works a little differently from, but is also similar to, SVN. We already installed the EGit plug-in, so we don't need to worry about that anymore.

The basic principles are the same as with SVN: you have a view specifically for Git and you can commit, update, and merge files from the team menu. Let's see how that works.

Open up the Git Repositories view. You will see a bunch of icons (Figure 2-4).

Next we'll go over how to make a local repository to which you can commit and update in order to illustrate that Git does not need an Internet connection to work. This is one of the powers of Git, and it makes it incredibly fast.

Figure 2-4. The Git Repositories view icon bar

Hover over the third icon, the one with the yellow plus sign (+); you should see the message "Create a new Git repository and add it to this view." Click the icon, give the repository a location and a name, and click Finish, and we are done (see Figure 2-5).

Figure 2-5. Creating a Git repository in your workspace

Now we can start adding files to our repository. For demonstration purposes, I copied over the *src* folder from our sample project. Once you have added source files, refresh the Git view to show them. Switch over to the FDT view and right-click anywhere in the Flash Explorer window or go to File→Import. From here, select Git→"Projects from Git." This should show us myCoolProject. Select it and click Next. Select "Import as General Project" and click Next again. Review the final step and click Finish.

Now we have a Git repository as a new project in Eclipse, but we still need to make it a Flash project, just like we did with SVN. So, right-click on the project to add the Flash nature, select the SDK and project type, and again add the *src* folder to the classpath. Ta-da! A fully functional Flash project under Git versioning!

Go ahead and open up the *Main.as* file and add a comment. As you can see, Git has a different way of showing you that there is a change to the file. Instead of icons, it displays a greater-than sign (>) before the filename.

Select the *src* folder, right-click it, and select Team. You'll see you have different options because we are now targeting Git. Select the commit option, and you should get the dialog shown in Figure 2-6.

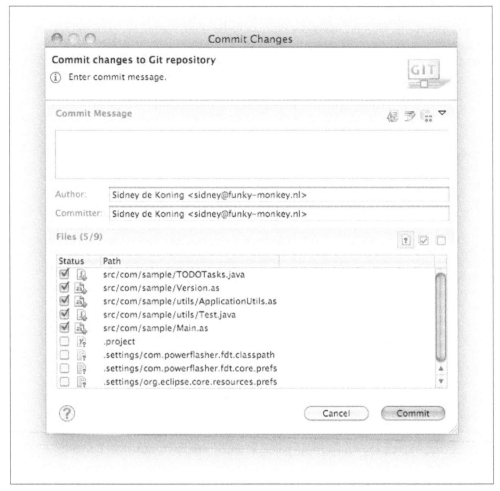

Figure 2-6. Committing file changes to a Git repository

Type in your commit message and click Commit.

If you go back to the Git Repository view, right-click the *src* folder, and select "Show in history," you will see a log of all the commits made and all the files that were affected.

Congratulations! You've successfully set up SVN and Git repositories, handled basic versioning commands like committing and updating files, and learned the inner workings of a version control system.

## CHAPTER 3

Automation

Ant

Now let's dive into Ant, which stands for Another Neat Tool. Ant was actually created as a *build scripting language* for Java development, but because it can be easily extended, it can also be used for other languages. Ant can help you automate your daily development tasks, including but not limited to compiling, testing, packaging, deploying, and documenting. Everything you can do with the command line—and more—you can do with Ant! You can also run Ant directly from the command line, but for the exercises in this book we will be running Ant only from within Eclipse.

Ant is a *task-oriented build system*, which means it allows you to create tasks and run them in a linear way—i.e., one after another. But, of course, tasks—or *targets*, as Ant calls them—can have dependencies on other tasks.

Before we can start playing around with Ant, we need to make sure we have all the JAR files in place and set up.

 JAR files are Java ARchives, a way to distribute source code or libraries. These files hold different files, ranging from source code to images and text files.

I have prepared a zip file with all the JAR files you'll need for this book. You can find it at *http://book.funky-monkey.nl/*. Just unpack this zip somewhere on your hard drive where you see fit.

Now open up Eclipse's preferences and click on the Ant options on the left side. Select the checkbox for "Always run new Ant config..." (Figure 3-1). Checking this option ensures that we don't have to select the Java runtime every time we create or use a new Ant build file. It also minimizes errors we get when compiling the Ant build file (one of the most common sources of errors).

Now select Runtime. Choose Global Entries and click Add External JARs (Figure 3-2).

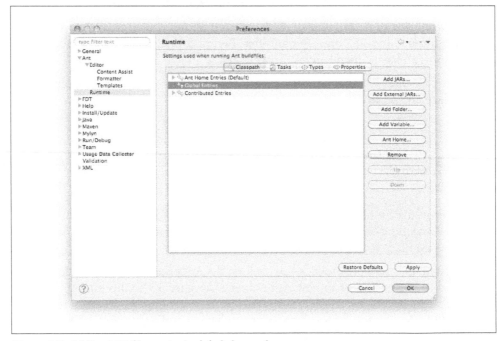

Figure 3-1. Common problems: running in a different JRE

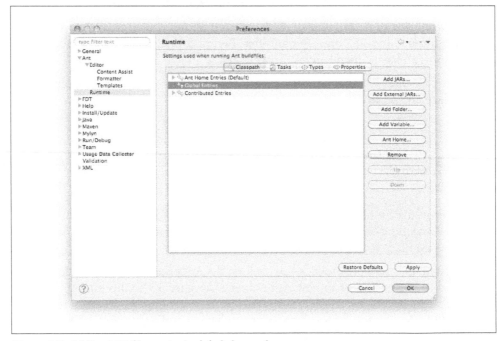

Figure 3-2. Adding JAR files to Ant's global classpath

Now point the file browser to the directory where you extracted all those JAR files. You can select multiple files at once; you don't have to do them one by one. Once you have added them, you should see something like the screen shown in Figure 3-3.

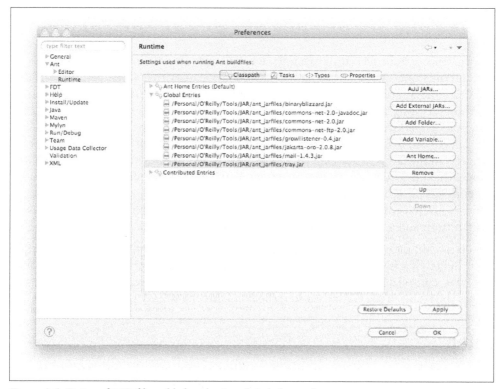

Figure 3-3. External JAR files added to the Ant global classpath

Click OK. Congratulations! We are all set. Now it's time to dive into the actual Ant scripts.

The Basics

Ant uses an XML syntax for its build files. A typical Ant file looks like this:

```
<project name="MyProject" default="compile" basedir=".">
    <target name="init">
        <tstamp/>
        <mkdir dir="build"/>
    </target>
    <target name="compile" depends="init" description="compile the source" >
        <javac srcdir="src" destdir="build"/>
    </target>
</project>
```

Even if you have no prior experience with Ant, it is very easy to read and understand.

 A build file is an XML file, usually called *build.xml*, with a collection of functions and variables (or targets and properties, as Ant calls them).

If we go through the preceding example, we see one project definition. (An Ant file can contain only one.) Its default is set to "compile," meaning that when you run this file, the first function or target that runs is the compile target. The name of a target can be anything, as long as it is a string of text and numbers. So using "1 - My very cool function" is perfectly legal. (I prefer a long, descriptive target name, because it makes it easier to read in Eclipse's Ant panel. But, if you prefer, you can also add a description property in the target to describe what that target does. The downside here is that when you let that target depend on another target, you have to type out its full name. But I'll cover this topic more later.) The compile target has a depends property, which is set to "init." This, in turn, runs the init target before it runs the compile target. It also creates a timestamp and a directory with the name *build*.

When the init target finishes executing, it moves back to the compile target. This then uses the newly created directory to compile a Java project using *javac* (the command-line Java compiler) with all the files located in the source directory (called *src*) and places the result of the compilation in the *build* directory. Easy peasy lemon squeezy!

Setup

I'm a visual thinker, so things always become clearer to me when I draw out the elements I want to create or code. I prefer to have a system give me visual feedback, which is why I always start my Ant files with a better method to trace out the information for debugging.

My basic setup includes a way to trace my message to Growl. Growl is a notification system that other programs can hook into and make use of. It offers both Mac and Windows versions. Growl can "listen" for incoming connections, and that is exactly what we would like it to do here. Open up Growl's preferences, click on the Network tab, and check the "Listen for incoming notifications" option (Figure 3-4).

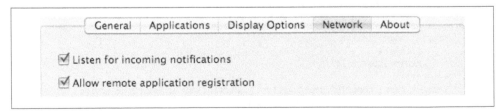

Figure 3-4. Allowing Growl to listen to incoming connections

Since we added the *binaryblizzard.jar* and *growllistener-0.4.jar* files to Ant's classpath, we can now make use of them by calling the *taskdef* in the Ant file. Taskdef is basically an import statement that you can call with a function name and a reference to a class name. The following line makes the task `growl` available for Ant to use by implementing it from the `net.slimeslurp.growl.GrowlEcho` class:

```
<taskdef name="growl" classname="net.slimeslurp.growl.GrowlEcho" />
```

Now open the OS X Terminal utility and type:

```
set ANT_ARGS=-listener net.slimeslurp.growl.GrowlListener
```

This ensures that Growl can listen to notifications coming from Ant. It is always a good idea to restart your system after doing this.

Now for the code: I start with this template for almost every Ant project, depending on what I'm building. Different projects require different methods of tracing:

```
<?xml version="1.0" encoding="UTF-8"?>
    <project name="Default Project" basedir=".">
    <taskdef name="growl" classname="net.slimeslurp.growl.GrowlEcho" />
    <!-- Create timestamp for filename. Format like so: 09/24/2009 05:33:22 PM -->
<target name="Creates a Timestamp">
        <tstamp>
            <format property="current.date.time"  pattern="dd_MM_yyyy_HH_mm" />
        </tstamp>
        <growl message="Custom Time format time stamp: ${current.date.time}" />
        </target>
</project>
```

This creates a timestamp and traces out its value using Growl. Pretty neat, eh? Now we can use this template for every Ant build we create.

Now that we have the basics down, let's move on to something more useful.

Our First "Real" Ant Script

Next, we will use our new template to create our first real Ant script.

To get you started, I will explain some of the fundamentals of the Ant language. These are the basic functions you need to learn for now; along the way, we will explore more, so don't worry when we don't cover them all at once.

Projects

Every Ant XML file starts off with an XML declaration (for good practice) and a project begin node and end node. The *project node* is kind of like a target, except that there can be only one. For it to function properly, it needs to have a `name` property. The `basedir` property defines the directory Ant should start from—for example, when it needs to traverse directories. The following is an example of a project node:

```xml
<?xml version="1.0" encoding="UTF-8"?>
    <project name="Default Project" basedir=".">
        ...
    </project>
```

 If you need to go one directory level higher, you can use either `../../`
or `.`; just make sure you also place your Ant build file in the root of your
Eclipse project.

Functions

As mentioned previously, Ant calls functions *targets*. A target consists of a target node
with a `name` element. This element is mandatory, meaning it must always be in a target.
The `name` element is basically the name of your target, and it enables you to call that
target via the command line from a build file. You can also add a `description` property
to describe what the target does, as shown here:

```xml
<target name="create-timestamp" description="Creates a Timestamp">
    ...
</target>
```

Running an Ant script in Eclipse is easy. Just open the Ant View (Window→Show
View→Ant), drag your Ant file in there, and double-click the main file. That way, it
runs the default target defined in the `default` property in the project node. If you unfold
the XML, you can see all your targets and run them separately. It should look something
like Figure 3-5. Select one and double-click it.

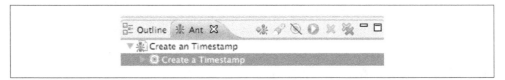

Figure 3-5. Ant target in an Eclipse view

When you run this Ant script by double-clicking it, its output looks something like
Figure 3-6.

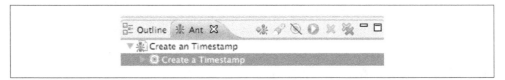

Figure 3-6. Ant build successful

Variables

Ant can also store variables or read out properties. As with every scripting or programming language, it's bad practice to hardcode values in Ant.

How does Ant handle variables? First, Ant has a bunch of built-in properties that can come in handy when you're creating build scripts. We already saw one, `basedir`, but there are more. Here is a (partial) list:

`ant.file`
> The absolute path of the build file

`ant.project.name`
> The name of the project as set in the project node

`ant.home`
> The root directory of Ant

`ant.version`
> The version of this Ant installation

`ant.java.version`
> The version of Java that Ant uses

`basedir`
> The absolute path of the project

`os.name`
> Operating system name

`os.arch`
> Operating system architecture

`os.version`
> Operating system version

`file.separator`
> File separator (/ on *nix and \ on Windows)

`path.separator`
> Path separator (: on *nix)

`line.separator`
> Line separator (\n on *nix)

`java.home`
> Java home directory name

`user.home`
> User directory name

`user.name`
> Username as set by login name on OS

`user.dir`
> User's current working directory

You can call these within your build file by using `${os.version}`; Ant uses the `${}` syntax to read properties. Just remember that a variable or property exists only during the complete build cycle. So once the build is completed, that variable does not exist anymore.

 You can find more of these built-in properties on Ant's documentation site:*http://ant.apache.org/manual/index.html*.

So now you know how to *get* properties, but how do you *set* them? You can set them during runtime or by using a property file. (It is common practice with Ant to give your variables or properties a name containing dots.) In the following example, we set them at runtime:

```
<property name="my.first.property" value="yay" />
<property name="my.second.property" value="1.1" />
```

Or like so (I used this example before):

```
<format property="current.date.time" pattern="dd_MM_yyyy_HH_mm" />
```

What we've done is assign the variable name (or set the property) `current.date.time` to hold the value of the timestamp, formatted in a specific way.

The second option for setting properties is by using a property file—just a plain-text file containing values. The benefit of using this method is that your code does not hold hardcoded references to paths or any other specific information. Property files almost always end with *.properties*—for example, *deploy.properties*, *ftp.properties*, *compile.properties*, *sdk.properties*, *local.properties*, etc. You can have as many as you want or place all the information in one *build.properties* file; it's up to you.

Here is an example of a *build.properties* file:

```
# Deploy directories
project.dir.build=build
project.dir.lib=lib
project.dir.src=src
project.dir.docs=docs
project.dir.tests=tests
project.dir.deploy=deploy
project.dir.zip=zip

# Flash output
project.dir.swc=swc

# Flash output
project.user=${user.name}
```

As you can see, you can insert comments using the pound sign (#).

 Using # to indicate comments can be done only in property files, not in build files. In build files, you use normal JavaScript-/XML-style comments, like so: `<!-- Sample Comment -->`.

So, again, if you want to use *project.dir.swc*, you would use `${project.dir.swc}` in your build XML file, or use built-in or custom-created properties directly in your property file itself.

To make use of a property file within your build file, you have to *include* it, or make a reference to it. You can do so like this:

```
<project>
    <property file="build.properties" />
    ...
```

Here, *build.properties* is just a text file (with *.properties* as its extension) with the properties in it, as described previously.

So, if we were to put this into practice, the code would be something like the following. We create two files: *build.properties* and *build.xml*. After you are done, compile the script. Here are the contents of the *build.properties* file:

```
# Project Properties
project.name=My_Project
```

And here are the contents of *build.xml*:

```
<?xml version="1.0" encoding="UTF-8"?>
<project name="Create Timestamp for filename" basedir=".">

    <taskdef name="growl" classname="net.slimeslurp.growl.GrowlEcho"/>

    <!-- Load project.properties file -->
    <property file="build.properties" />

    <!-- Create timestamp for filename. Format like so: 09/24/2009 05:33:22 PM -->
    <target name="create-timestamp" description="Create a timestamp">
        <tstamp>
            <format property="current.date.time" pattern="dd_MM_yyyy_HH_mm" />
        </tstamp>
        <growl message="Current date / time ${current.date.time}" />
    </target>
</project>
```

You should see the output shown in Figure 3-7 from the Eclipse console. If you see this, you know everything went according to plan.

Figure 3-7. Ant has been built without problems

At the same time, you should see a notification from Growl (Figure 3-8).

Figure 3-8. Growl notification from Ant

The most common error you can encounter is that the Ant Java runtime runs in a different JRE than Eclipse. You can set the JRE globally in Eclipse's Ant preferences, as we did in the beginning of this chapter, or you can set it per build file.

The error message reads "BUILD FAILED: Could not create task or type." You can solve this by right-clicking the actual *build.xml* file and selecting Run As→"External Tools configuration." Go to the JRE tab and select "Run in the same JRE as the workspace" (Figure 3-9).

 Ant's documentation includes an FAQ section that also discusses Ant's most common errors. You can find it online at *http://ant.apache.org/faq .html.*

Congratulations—you just created your first useful Ant build script! Now let's delve into hooking up Ant with FDT.

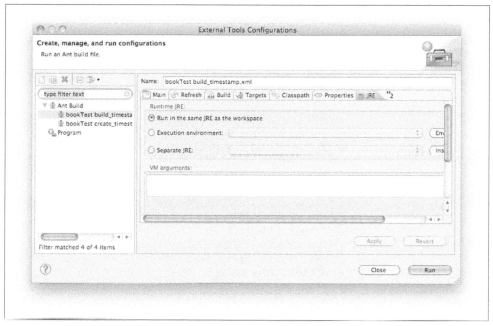

Figure 3-9. Always run in the same JRE.

Directly Calling the Compiler

When you're developing in FDT, there are a few ways to compile your ActionScript projects: calling the compiler directly from the Flex SDK, compiling directly from FDT, or combining both approaches.

You are free to use the method you prefer—whichever gives you more freedom to do what you want. I will go through each of them.

You can directly call the compiler or make use of FDT's internal Ant tasks (more on the latter option in "Using FDT's Ant Tasks" on page 41).

 When you want to call the compiler directly, you need to have a copy of the Flex SDK, which can be found at Adobe's open source site: *http: //opensource.adobe.com/wiki/display/flexsdk/Downloads*.

Downloading the Flex SDK

Installing an SDK is easy: just download and extract the files. I place mine in the root of my hard drive in a folder called *SDK* and differentiate them by version number, as shown in Figure 3-10.

Figure 3-10. Organized folder structure with all SDKs

This way, I have all the SDKs I need, neatly organized in one folder (also a time-saver!). Once you have extracted the SDK, you need to go over to FDT and add the new SDK.

If you haven't done so already, create a new AS3 project in FDT by going to File→New→New Flash Project, and give it a name you prefer. You can change the SDK used by right-clicking on the newly created project (the blue folder with the big F in it) and selecting Flash Project→Change SDK. You are now presented with a dialog box. Press Configure on the right.

You can add your own SDK by clicking Add (Figure 3-11). Now search for the extracted SDK on your hard drive. FDT will automatically look for all the SWCs related to this SDK and set up everything you need (Figure 3-12).

Click OK and go back to your project. Again, right-click and select Flash Project→Select Project Type. Here, choose AS3 4.5 from the drop-down list and then select the SDK you just added (Figure 3-13).

You are now ready to start using your newly added SDK with your project.

Compiling

Now we want an Ant build to directly call the compiler, so we create a new XML file by pressing Command-N and typing **xml**. Select XML, give it a name, and click Finish. To keep things organized, place the file in the root folder of your project or in a folder called *ant*. After you've done this, open the file and start with the contents of the template we created earlier.

Figure 3-11. Selecting the correct SDK

First things first: we create a new property file called *sdk.properties* and also place it in the *ant* directory. This file will include the path of the SDK and the path to the actual compiler. The reason we create a separate file for this is that the location of the SDK is machine-specific.

Creating our own standard ensures that we can always look in one place rather than go to line number *x* in one file somewhere in that directory. "Short and clear," as my mentor used to say. It is also easier to extend if, for example, we want to compile to AIR, Android, or iPhone with different SDKs to use in one project. Now there is one centralized place to make modifications. We will use this standard throughout the rest of these exercises.

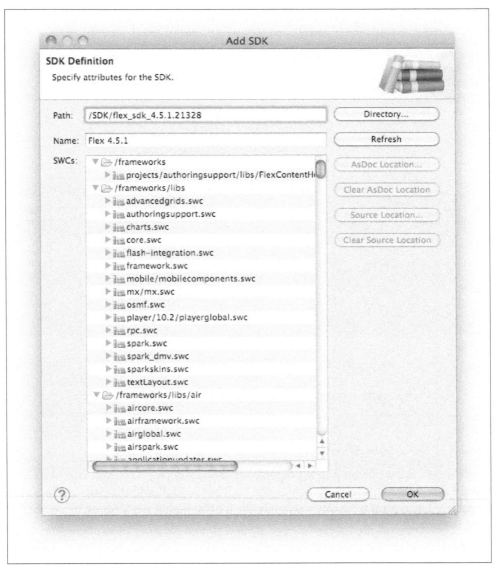

Figure 3-12. The Flex SDK content

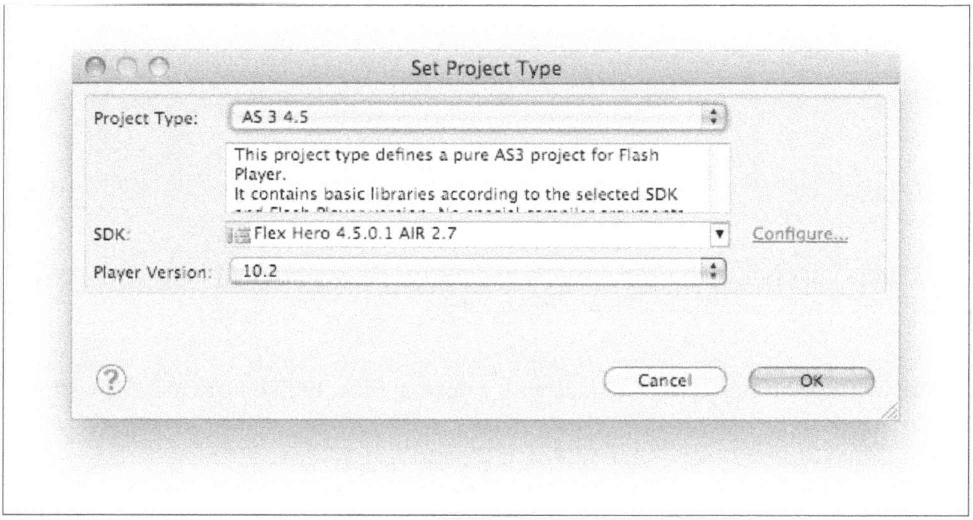

Figure 3-13. Selecting the correct project type

Here are the contents of this file (notice the use of the ${file.separator}; this is operating system–specific):

```
# SDK Properties
sdk.location=${file.separator}SDK${file.separator}flex_sdk_4.5.0.18623
sdk.libs.framework=${sdk.location}${file.separator}frameworks
sdk.libs.location=${sdk.libs.framework}${file.separator}libs
sdk.mxmlc.compiler=${sdk.location}${file.separator}lib${file.separator}mxmlc.jar
```

The next file you will create in the *ant* directory is called *build.properties*, and it holds information about the actual project we are compiling:

```
# Project Properties
project.name=My_Project
project.document.class=Main.as
project.src.path=${basedir}${file.separator}src
project.bin.path=${basedir}${file.separator}bin
project.debug.path==${basedir}${file.separator}debug project.deploy.path=${basedir}
${file.separator}deploy
project.assets.path=${basedir}${file.separator}assets
project.classpath=${project.src.path}${file.separator}com${file.separator}sample
${file.separator}
```

To test whether we got the right paths, we create a small target to trace out these values. Since we are on a Mac, the file (or path) separator will be replaced with the appropriate slash (as we saw earlier in the chapter, in the list of commonly used default properties).

As you can see from the preceding example, we also created the folder structure shown in Figure 3-14.

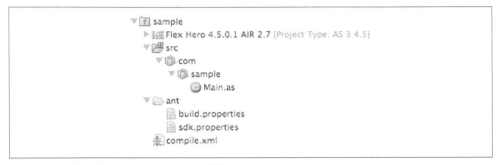

Figure 3-14. Sample project directory and file structure

For all intents and purposes, we trace with a normal echo, but you can use Growl if you wish:

```
<target name="trace" description="Trace out path properties">
    <echo message="SDK Location : ${sdk.location}" />
    <echo message="SDK Libs Compiler : ${sdk.mxmlc.compiler}" />
    <echo message="SDK Libs Loc : ${sdk.libs.location}" />
    <echo message="Classpath : ${project.classpath}" />
    <echo message="BaseDir : ${basedir}" />
</target>
```

The resulting echo looks something like the following:

```
[echo] SDK Location : /SDK/flex_sdk_4.5.0.18623
[echo] SDK Libs Compiler :/SDK/flex_sdk_4.5.0.18623/lib/mxmlc.jar
[echo] SDK Libs Loc : /SDK/flex_sdk_4.5.0.18623/frameworks/libs
[echo] Classpath : /Personal/O'Reilly/Tools/workspace/sample/src/com/sample/
[echo] BaseDir : /Personal/O'Reilly/Tools/workspace/sample
BUILD SUCCESSFUL
Total time: 234 milliseconds
```

You can see how incredibly fast it is to compile with Ant.

Let's go inside the *Main.as* file before we start the actual compiling. *Main.as* is a very simple ActionScript file that creates a square on a black background. We set the background color, frame rate, width, and height of the outputted SWF with the supplied meta injection code within the brackets:

```
package com.sample {
    import flash.display.Sprite;

    [SWF(backgroundColor="#000000", frameRate="31", width="200", height="200")]

    public class Main extends Sprite {

        public function Main() {
            var s:Sprite = new Sprite();
            s.graphics.beginFill(0xff00aa, 1);
            s.graphics.drawRect(50, 50, 100, 100);
            s.graphics.endFill();
            addChild(s);
```

```
        }
    }
}
```

We start off with the project template we already used, and add some extra code to compile the SWF:

```
<target name="compile" description="Compile a SWF with MXMLC Compiler" depends="create-
timestamp">
    <java jar="${sdk.mxmlc.compiler}" fork="true" failonerror="true">
        <arg value="-debug=false" />
        <arg value="-optimize=true" />
        <arg value="-verbose-stacktraces=true" />
        <arg value="+flexlib=${sdk.libs.framework}" />
        <arg value="-source-path=${project.src.path}" />
        <arg value="-library-path=${sdk.libs.location}" />
        <arg value="-file-specs=${project.classpath}${project.document.class}
${project.file.extension}" />
        <arg value="-output=${project.bin.path}${file.separator}
${project.document.class}_${current.date.time}.swf" />
    </java>
    <eclipse.refreshLocal resource="${project.name}" depth="infinite" />
</target>
```

Here, you see we introduce a new target called java. With this target, we can execute the code inside a JAR file—and that is exactly what we want to do.

We can also add a couple of extra parameters. We only use the parameters jar, failonerror, and fork. failonerror will stop the build process if there is an error, and must be used in conjunction with fork to allow execution of other classes in a forked VM (virtual machine). With the jar parameter, we can pass the JAR file location for the actual compiling to SWF.

> For a full list of passable parameters, see *http://ant.apache.org/manual/Tasks/java.html*.

The nested arg property allows us to pass extra arguments to the JAR file's execution.

A little explanation on the arguments passed: -debug makes sure we are not using the debugger, -optimize compresses the outputted SWF, and -verbose-stacktraces gives us more detailed information if something breaks while we're running the SWF (i.e., runtime errors).

> Some loggers, like Trazzle (*http://www.nesium.com/products/trazzle*), actually need you to set the -verbose-stacktraces=true compiler argument so you can log to them.

We now have our *sdk.properties*, *build.properties*, *compile.xml*, and *Main.as* written. If we run the compile target, everything should go as planned and create the actual SWF file in the *bin* directory. The `eclipse.refreshLocal` target makes sure the directory in our workspace is refreshed after it's been compiled. This is an Ant task that is bundled with Eclipse.

If, for some reason, you have an error in your AS file, the mxmlc compiler will catch it and give you a descriptive error message. If we, for instance, look at the line where we add the sprite to the stage, rename **s** to **a**, and compile again, we will get the following error message:

```
compile:
[java] /src/com/sample/Main.as(15): col: 13 Error: Access of undefined property a.
[java]           addChild(a);
[java]                    ^
```

You will see the filename of the class with the compiler error, the line number, and the actual position with a description. Now go back to fix it, and compile again.

Adding external SWC libraries

If you make use of external libraries in an SWC format, you would include them with an extra argument, just above the closing of the final Java tag:

```
<arg value="-l+=${project.libs.path}" />
```

And you would also add the following in the *build.properties* file:

```
project.libs.path=${basedir}${file.separator}libs
```

Cleaning

The last thing we are going to add to our *compile.xml* file is a clean target. It is very good practice to clean up after yourself. Every build file should include a clean target to remove all the generated directories and files, thereby bringing it back to its original state. We also include a call to the `eclipse.refreshLocal` target to see the changes in our workspace once the target has executed:

```
<target name="clean" description="Purge the contents of the bin dir">
    <delete dir="${project.bin.path}"/>
    <delete dir="${project.debug.path}"/>
    <eclipse.refreshLocal resource="${project.name}" depth="infinite" />
</target>
```

 Eric M. Burke wrote a really good article, "Top 15 Ant Best Practices," for O'Reilly in 2003. Providing a clean target is #5 on that list. I strongly encourage you to read it: *http://tim.oreilly.com/pub/a/onjava/2003/12/17/ant_bestpractices.html*.

Debugging

Debugging is as simple as changing -debug=false to -debug=true, and the path of the directory to the debug path set in *build.properties*. So, the code then becomes:

```
<target name="debug" description="Debug a SWF with MXMLC Compiler" depends="create-
timestamp">
    <java jar="${sdk.mxmlc.compiler}" fork="true" failonerror="true">
        <arg value="-debug=true" />
        <arg value="-optimize=true" />
        <arg value="-verbose-stacktraces=true" />
        <arg value="+flexlib=${sdk.libs.framework}" />
        <arg value="-source-path=${project.src.path}" />
        <arg value="-library-path=${sdk.libs.location}" />
        <arg value="-file-specs=${project.classspath}${project.document.class}
${project.file.extension}" />
        <arg value="-output=${project.debug.path}${file.separator}
${project.document.class}_DEBUG_${current.date.time}.swf" />
    </java>
    <eclipse.refreshLocal resource="${project.name}" depth="infinite" />
</target>
```

Using FDT's Ant Tasks

When you're using FDT, there are a lot of specific Ant tasks you can hook into or use to make compiling and debugging even simpler.

At the time of this writing, here is the complete list of Ant tasks for FDT (there will probably be more implemented in the future, as FDT is being developed really quickly):

- fdt.loadProjectProperties (only from FDT 4.1 and up)
- fdt.browse
- fdt.extSWFViewer.focusWindow
- fdt.extSWFViewer.startSWF
- fdt.flashCompile
- fdt.launch.application
- fdt.launch.library
- fdt.launch.resetFlexCompiler
- fdt.startDebugger
- fdt.startProfiler

FDT works with *launchers*, which are basically shortcuts for viewing your project in a specific version of the Flash Player. You can use them when calling the swflauncher argument with your Ant targets. Here is the list of launchers you can use with FDT:

- External SWF Viewer
- Adobe Flash Player

- Browser
- Internal SWF Viewer
- AIR Debug Launcher

The first built-in FDT Ant task we'll look at is `fdt.launch.application`. With this task, you can compile, debug, and profile your application. Let's take a look first at compiling.

Compiling (with FDT Ant Tasks)

Compiling with FDT Ant tasks is a bit simpler than directly calling the compiler:

```
<target name="compile-fdt" description="Compile a SWF with FDT Ant Tasks"
depends="create-timestamp">
    <fdt.launch.application
        debug="false"
        projectname="${FDTProject}"
    mainclass="${project.classpath}${project.document.class}${project.file.extension}"
        target="${project.bin.path}${file.separator}${project.document.class}_$
{current.date.time}.swf"
        compilerarguments="-verbose-stacktraces=true"
        startswf="true"
        swflauncher="External SWF Viewer"/>
    <eclipse.refreshLocal resource="${project.name}" depth="infinite" />
</target>
```

(The downside of using this method is that if you want to distribute your *build.xml* file, everyone has to have FDT installed. When directly calling the compiler, you don't run into this problem.)

Looking at this code, you see it does exactly the same thing as calling the compiler directly—it's only written differently. If you look more closely, you'll see that we brought in a new property: `FDTProject`. By default, FDT has a set of built-in properties that we can use; here is the complete list:

`${FDTProject}`
    Returns the name of the project

`${FDTProjectPath}`
    Returns the path of the project

`${FDTProjectSdkPath}`
    Returns the path of the current SDK

`${FDTProjectSdkName}`
    Returns the name of the current SDK

`${FDTProjectSdkVersion}`
    Returns the version of the SDK, written in full

`${FDTProjectPlayerVersion}`
    Returns the Flash Player version used in the project

`${FDTProjectKind}`
> Returns the type of project (e.g., Flash Player, AIR)

`${FDTHostIP}`
> Returns the host IP for the debugger to connect to

Before we can use these properties in our project, we must make a call at the top of our build file (we do this at the top because our build file is read from top to bottom):

```
<!-- Load project.properties file -->
<property file="ant${file.separator}build.properties" />
<property file="ant${file.separator}sdk.properties" />
<fdt.loadProjectProperties/>
```

Then we do a quick echo of all these properties, so you can see that they return the correct values. This should give you something similar to the following list:

```
[echo] sample
[echo] /Personal/O'Reilly/Tools/workspace/sample
[echo] /SDK/flex_sdk_4.5.1.21328
[echo] Flex 4.5.1
[echo] 4.5.1.21328
[echo] 10.2
[echo] Flash Player
[echo] 192.168.0.194
```

Debugging (with FDT Ant Tasks)

Debugging is a bit different than normal compiling, and it is not included with every version of FDT. You can debug only if you have the Max version.

 For more information on the different versions of FDT, see *http://www .fdt.powerflasher.com/developer-tools/fdt/features/*.

If you have the Max version, proceed as follows. First, we need to call the debugger with `fdt.startDebugger` with the correct project name. We do this just as we did with the compiling—with `${FDTProject}`. Then, we set `switchperspectiveonbreakpoint` to true. Now, when we set a breakpoint in our code (by double-clicking on the line gutter at that specific point), FDT actually switches to the Debugger View and introspects the code on that breakpoint.

The default for this option is true, so you only have to set it explicitly if you *don't* want to use it:

```
<target name="debug-fdt" description="Debug a SWF with FDT Ant Tasks" depends="create-
timestamp">
    <fdt.startDebugger
        projectname="${FDTProject}"
        switchperspectiveonbreakpoint="true"
```

```
    />
    <fdt.launch.application
        debug="true"
        projectname="${FDTProject}"
        mainclass="${project.classpath}${project.document.class}$
{project.file.extension}"
        target="${project.debug.path}${file.separator}${project.document.class}_DEBUG_
${current.date.time}.swf"
        compilerarguments="-verbose-stacktraces=true"
        startswf="true"
        swflauncher="External SWF Viewer"
    />
    <eclipse.refreshLocal resource="${project.name}" depth="infinite" />
</target>
```

After calling `fdt.startDebugger`, we call `fdt.launch.application` like we did when we were compiling, only now we set the `debug` flag to `true`, change the target directory to output in our *debug* folder, and add *_DEBUG_* to the filename of the outputted SWF file to differentiate between a debugged SWF and a nondebugged SWF (just like we did when we called the compiler directly).

Deploying Your SWF Files to a Different Source

One of the cool features of Ant is that you are not bound to only doing local development. You can also deploy and/or copy your files to a web server, FTP server, or a network share.

Let's start with an inventory of what we need when we want to test on a web server:

- An HTML file that embeds our SWF file
- The JavaScript embed method via SWFObject (*http://code.google.com/p/swfob ject/*)
- A specific folder structure so that everything is neatly organized

That's it! So what are we actually going to do? We have all the needed project properties defined in our property file. With those, we can build a directory structure and generate our actual HTML file. We do this with Ant so we don't have to do it by hand for every project we do. This is a huge time-saver!

We are actually going to change our build files a little bit. Because deploying is a different process than compiling and debugging, I prefer to work in a different file called *deploy.xml*.

The benefit of using separate files is that the functionality defined in the filename is neatly encapsulated in one file—there's no searching required, since the name says it all. Each file can be easily distributed to freelancers or colleagues who are setting up the builds on their machines.

Let's start editing our *build.xml* file, and strip out everything except loading Growl, loading our properties, and creating the timestamp target:

```xml
<?xml version="1.0" encoding="UTF-8"?>
<project name="Main Build file" basedir=".">
    <!-- Import Growl Classes so we can send notifications via Growl -->
    <taskdef name="growl" classname="net.slimeslurp.growl.GrowlEcho" />

    <!-- Load project.properties file -->
    <buildnumber file="ant/${project.name}.number"/>
    <property file="ant/build.properties" />
    <property file="ant/sdk.properties" />
    <fdt.loadProjectProperties/>

    <!-- Create timestamp for filename. Format like so: 09/24/2009 05:33:22
        PM -->
    <target name="create-timestamp" description="Create a timestamp">
        <tstamp>
            <format property="current.date.time" pattern="dd_MM_yyyy_HH_mm" />
        </tstamp>
        <growl message="Current date / time ${current.date.time}" />
    </target>
</project>
```

In the *compile_fdt.xml* we created earlier, we strip out only the timestamp target and replace that with the import to our *build.xml*. So the top of the file looks like this.

```xml
<?xml version="1.0" encoding="UTF-8"?>
<project name="Compiling Flash Project with FDT Tasks" basedir=".">

    <!-- Import all properties etc. -->
    <import file="build.xml" as="build"/>
```

We do the same thing for *compile.xml*.

In *compile_fdt.xml* and *compile.xml*, we can now call the timestamp target, but we need to call it from our imported *build.xml*. The import task has an **as** property for exactly that reason—to call a function/target from another file. We create an alias so we don't have to call *build.xml* every time.

So, if we call `build.create-timestamp` from within this file, we are calling the *build.xml* file's `create-timestamp` target.

Last, in both files (*compile.xml* and *compile_fdt.xml*), we change the lines:

```xml
<target name="compile-fdt" ... depends="create-timestamp">
```

and:

```xml
<target name="debug-fdt" ... depends="create-timestamp">
```

to:

```xml
<target name="compile-fdt" ... depends="build.create-timestamp">
```

and:

```
<target name="debug-fdt" ... depends="build.create-timestamp">
```

Now we are done with the hard part! You've also learned two valuable practices: importing other build files and calling targets from them.

Setting Up Web Deployment

Adding Information to a SWF

Whether you're debugging or just compiling, it is always good practice to have some sort of info panel in your SWF. What do I mean by *info panel*? This can be an actual overlay or context menu with profiling information, memory usage, build/compile version, the user who compiled that version, and more.

One of the easiest ways to implement an info panel in AS3 is by using the context menu or right-click menu.

 If you need a good, basic visual profiler, I highly recommend Shane McCartney's SWF Profiler Class. It shows your SWF's memory usage and frames per second in a very visual manner. For more information, see *http://lostinactionscript.com/2008/10/06/as3-swf-profiler/*.

Since this class is open source, it can also be a good base on which to write your own extension.

Why do we want to add an info panel? Consider the following case: you're testing a project you've been working on with a team, a client, or maybe open source collaborators. But what version was deployed online yesterday? And who uploaded it? And at what time was it created?

An info panel saves you time and energy by enabling you to just right-click on the SWF in that web page—no more opening an FTP connection to find out what time the file was uploaded and other relevant information.

What do we want to accomplish? We want a context menu that shows us information about a file's date, operating version, and build number; which user compiled it; and a line indicating your company name with a link to your site.

What we need is a generated *Version.as* file, an *ApplicationsUtils.as* file, and adjustments to our *Main.as* document class.

Let's start with the Ant target to generate the *Version.as* file in the correct location. As you can see, we can use the echo task not only to trace out information about our build process, but also to write Ant text or information to a file. We will discuss this a little bit more in the next example for generating the HTML file.

For the echo file output to work, we use the format file="*location of file to be*":

```
<target name="0.generate-info-class" description="Create an info class that show
information when right clikced in the SWF" depends="build.create-timestamp">
    <echo file="${project.classpath}Version${project.file.extension}">
    package ${project.classpath.clean} {
        import flash.display.Sprite;
        import flash.events.ContextMenuEvent;
        import flash.ui.ContextMenu;
        import flash.ui.ContextMenuItem;
        import flash.net.URLRequest;
        import flash.net.navigateToURL;
        import ${project.classpath.clean}.utils.ApplicationUtils;

        /**
         * @author ${user.name}
         */
        public class Version
        {
            public static var DATE:String = "${current.date.time.readable}";
            public static var PROJECT_NAME:String = "${project.name}";
            public static var BUILT_ON:String = "${os.name} ${os.version}";
            public static var BUILD_NUMBER:String = "${build.number}";
            public static var USER_NAME:String = "${user.name}";

            public function Version( menuSprite : Sprite) {
                var cm : ContextMenu = new ContextMenu();
                cm.hideBuiltInItems();

                switch(ApplicationUtils.getDevelopmentMode()) {

                    case ApplicationUtils.DEVELOPMENT:
                    // Do specific deveopment stuff here
cm.customItems.push(new ContextMenuItem("Project : " + Version.PROJECT_NAME));
cm.customItems.push(new ContextMenuItem("Date : " + Version.DATE));
cm.customItems.push(new ContextMenuItem("Built on : " + Version.BUILT_ON));
cm.customItems.push(new ContextMenuItem("Built by : " + Version.USER_NAME));
cm.customItems.push(new ContextMenuItem("Built # : " + Version.BUILD_NUMBER));

                    break;
                    case ApplicationUtils.PRODUCTION:
                    // Do specific production stuff here
cm.customItems.push(new ContextMenuItem("Project : " + Version.PROJECT_NAME));
cm.customItems.push(new ContextMenuItem("Date : " + Version.DATE));
cm.customItems.push(new ContextMenuItem("Built on : " + Version.BUILT_ON));
cm.customItems.push(new ContextMenuItem("Built # : " + Version.BUILD_NUMBER));
                    break;
                }

var notice : ContextMenuItem = new ContextMenuItem( "My Company Name, Year" );
notice.enabled = true;
notice.separatorBefore = true;
notice.addEventListener( ContextMenuEvent.MENU_ITEM_SELECT, menuItemSelect );

cm.customItems.push( notice );

menuSprite.contextMenu = cm;
```

```
                }

                private function menuItemSelect(evt : ContextMenuEvent) : void {
                    navigateToURL(new URLRequest("${remote.http.server}"));
                }
            }
        }
    </echo>
    <eclipse.refreshLocal resource="${project.name}" depth="infinite" />
</target>
```

For this example to work, we also need to add some properties to the usual place:

```
project.classpath.clean=com.sample
```

And since we implemented the `build.number` task, we can use `${build.number}` every-where in our build file. Every time the build file is run, this value gets incremented by one.

In our *build.xml* file, we need to adjust the timestamp function with a new property to output a new formatted timestamp, something that is human-readable. So, between the `tstamp` brackets, add the code shown in bold:

```
<tstamp>
    <format property ="current.date.time" pattern="dd_MM_yyyy_HH_mm" />
    <format property="current.date.time.readable" pattern="dd-MM-yyyy HH:mm" />
</tstamp>
```

Don't run this Ant target just yet. We need to add some more files to make this work properly. Next is our `ApplicationUtils` class.

If you are not in the FDT perspective anymore because you were editing XML files, switch back to it. Then, in FDT, create a new class in a new package called *utils* in the source folder. The classpath of this file becomes `com.sample.utils`.

This class will help you see if you are testing on a server or directly opening the SWF from FDT:

```
package com.sample.utils {
    import flash.display.DisplayObject;
    import flash.display.LoaderInfo;
    import flash.display.Sprite;

    /**
     * Example:
     * If you are testing your SWF file, you can find out if you are testing
     * online or locally and behave accordingly.
     *
     * The following example will set an XML file location by either getting
     * the FlashVar or manually load the XML file.
     * var xmlURL:String = ( ApplicationUtils.getDevelopmentMode( ) ==
ApplicationUtils.PRODUCTION ) ? ApplicationUtils.getFlashVars( ).xml : "./xml/
data.xml";
     *
     *
```

```
      */
    public class ApplicationUtils extends Sprite {

        public static const DEVELOPMENT : String = "Development";
        public static const PRODUCTION : String  = "Production";
        //
        private static var _docRoot : DisplayObject;
        private static var _topParent : DisplayObject;

        public static function init( docRoot : DisplayObject) : void {

            _docRoot = docRoot;
        }
        public static  function getFlashVars() : Object {
            return Object( getLoaderInfo(_docRoot).parameters );
        }

        public static  function getDevelopmentMode() : String {
    var dev : Boolean = new RegExp( "file://" ).test( _docRoot.loaderInfo.loaderURL );

            if( dev ) {
                return ApplicationUtils.DEVELOPMENT;
            } else {
                return ApplicationUtils.PRODUCTION;
            }
        }

        public static  function getContextPath() . String {
            var uri : String = getLoaderURL( );
            return uri.substring( 0, uri.lastIndexOf( "/" ) ) + "/";
        }

        public static function getLoaderURL() : String {
            return _docRoot.loaderInfo.loaderURL;
        }

        public static function getLoaderInfo(dispObj : DisplayObject) : LoaderInfo {
            var root : DisplayObject = getRootDisplayObject( dispObj );
            if (root != null) {
                return root.loaderInfo;
            }
            return null;
        }

        public static function getRootDisplayObject(dispObj : DisplayObject) :
DisplayObject {
            if (_topParent == null) {
                if (dispObj.parent != null) {
                    return getRootDisplayObject( dispObj.parent );
                } else {
                    _topParent = dispObj;
                    return _topParent;
                }
            } else {
                    return _topParent;
```

```
                }
            }
        }
    }
```

The last thing is to adjust the Main class:

```
package com.sample {
    import com.sample.utils.ApplicationUtils;

    import com.sample.Version;

    import flash.display.Sprite;
    import flash.display.StageAlign;
    import flash.display.StageQuality;
    import flash.display.StageScaleMode;
    import flash.events.Event;

    [SWF(backgroundColor="#000000", frameRate="31", width="200", height="200")]

    public class Main extends Sprite {
        public function Main() {
            addEventListener(Event.ADDED_TO_STAGE, handleAddedToStage);
        }

        private function start() : void {

            var s : Sprite = new Sprite();
            s.graphics.beginFill(0xff00aa, 1);
            s.graphics.drawRect(50, 50, 100, 100);
            s.graphics.endFill();
            addChild(s);
        }

        private function handleAddedToStage(event : Event) : void {

            stage.scaleMode = StageScaleMode.NO_SCALE;
            stage.align = StageAlign.TOP_LEFT;
            stage.quality = StageQuality.BEST;
            stage.stageFocusRect = false;

            init();
            start();
        }

        private function init() : void {
            // Init App utils for loader objects and flashvars
            ApplicationUtils.init(stage);

            // Add contextMenu with information
            var versionInfo : Version = new Version(this);
        }
    }
}
```

Now we are done; give yourself a well-deserved pat on the back! When you run the Ant target 0.generate-info-class, the Version.as class should be generated in the correct location.

The next time you compile to SWF, these newly created classes get compiled along with the existing ones because we placed them in the classpath. Also, remember to make sure this target gets called during each compile. You can do this by either creating a proxy target (a separate target that calls all the targets needed for compilation), or in the compile/debug target, calling this function using the depends parameter.

The implementation of all your hard work looks like Figure 3-15.

Figure 3-15. The custom right click menu in the Flash Player

Setting Up the HTML File

The standard practice is to test a Flash project or SWF within an HTML file. The big plus with this approach is that if we need to test using FlashVars, we can do so with relative ease from within the HTML. So next we will create an HTML file from scratch. We'll do this via the echo task in Ant, because it allows us to easily write to a file. But how do we automatically get the project properties in our HTML? Well, we are going to do something new here: work with tokens, and replace them with real values.

The advantage with token replacement is that we can work with template files— whether they are physically on the filesystem, or saved in properties/strings and generated with code. For now, we are choosing the latter.

The HTML we are creating has the following tokens:

- @html.title@
- @html.bgcolor@
- @html.width@
- @html.height@

These are placeholders for the code to be, which is the value we will replace using Ant so this can become a working HTML file. Of course, you can replace anything you want.

So, first, we need to create a target that will write the HTML. And since we want to distribute only the build files and property files, we want to try to generate as much as possible with Ant.

The way of embedding the SWF file in the HTML normally requires a JavaScript file called SWFObject. As of version 2, you can include this file straight from its repository, which means no more distributing extra unnecessary files. Just make a call to *http:// ajax.googleapis.com/ajax/libs/swfobject/2.2/swfobject.js*, and you can use it like you normally would.

 You can find more information about this method of embedding SWF files at *http://code.google.com/p/swfobject/wiki/hosted_library*.

```
<target name="1.generate-html-template">
    <echo output="${project.template.path}${file.separator}index.html" append="false">
        <![CDATA[<html>
            <head>
                <title>@html.title@</title>

                <style type="text/css" media="screen">
                    body {
                        margin:0; padding:0;
                        text-align:center;
                        background-color: #@html.bgcolor@;
                        font-family:Verdana, Arial, sans-serif;
                    }
                    #container {
                        margin:0px auto;
                        width:@html.width@px;
                        text-align:left;
                    }
                </style>
                <script
                    type="text/javascript"
                    language="javaScript"
                    src="http://ajax.googleapis.com/ajax/libs/swfobject/2.2/
swfobject.js"></script>
                <script type="text/javascript">
                    var flashvars  = {};

                    var params = {};
                    params.base = "static/swf";
                    params.allowScriptAccess = "always";

                    var attributes = {};
                    attributes.id = "application";
```

```
                    swfobject.embedSWF("static/swf/@html.swf.location@", "content",
    "@html.width@", "@html.height@", "10.0.0");

                </script>
            </head>
            <body>
                <div id="container">
                    <div id="content">
                        <h1>Alternative content</h1>
                        <p><a href="http://www.adobe.com/go/getflashplayer">
                        <img src="http://www.adobe.com/images/shared/download_buttons/
    get_flash_player.gif" alt="Get Adobe Flash player" /></a></p>
                    </div>
                </div>
            </body>
        </html>]]>
    </echo>
    <antcall target="2.replace-token" />
    <eclipse.refreshLocal resource="${project.name}" depth="infinite" />
</target>
```

As you can see, after the running of that target, we run another target to do the actual
token replacement:

```
<target name="2.replace-token" description="Do the actual replacing of tokens in
generated html file">
    <replace file="${project.template.path}${file.separator}index.html"
            propertyFile="ant${file.separator}build.properties">
        <replacefilter token="@html.title@" property="project.name"/>
        <replacefilter token="@html.bgcolor@" property="html.bgcolor"/>
        <replacefilter token="@html.width@" property="html.width"/>
        <replacefilter token="@html.height@" property="html.height"/>
    </replace>
    <!-- Since @html.swf.location@ is not defined in the property file, we need another
replace task -->
    <replace file="${project.template.path}${file.separator}index.html">
        <replacefilter token="@html.swf.location@" value="${project.output.swf}"/>
    </replace>
    <eclipse.refreshLocal resource="${project.name}" depth="infinite" />
</target>
```

Again, we need to refresh the workspace so we can see the changes made to folders and
files.

Now we have the compiled SWF with a timestamp, and our generated HTML with an
included JavaScript file from an online repository. The last thing we need to do is copy
it to our web server.

Next, we'll make minor adjustments to our *build.properties* file to store all the directories, our web server paths, and our username (but not our password). For this step,
we'll introduce a new type of Ant task: input. This allows us to gain input from the end
user, store it in a property, and use it later in the process (this property is stored only
during the build process):

```
project.web.path=${basedir}${file.separator}web
```

Now, we create a new property file called *remote.properties* and place within it the following:

```
#FTP Properties
remote.http.server=http://www.my-web-server.com/
remote.ftp.server=ftp.my-web-server.com
remote.ftp.port=21
remote.ftp.dir=/var/www/html/
remote.ftp.username=user@my-web-server.com
#passive    selects passive-mode ("yes") transfers, for better through-firewall
connectivity, at the price of performance. Defaults to "no"
remote.ftp.passivemode=yes
#verbose    displays information on each file transferred if set to "yes". Defaults
to "no".
remote.ftp.verbose=yes
#depends    transfers only new or changed files if set to "yes". Defaults to "no".
remote.ftp.depends=no
#binary selects binary-mode("yes") or text-mode ("no") transfers. Defaults to "yes"
remote.ftp.binary=yes
```

Don't forget to include this file at the top of the *deploy.xml* file, with:

```
<property file="ant${file.separator}remote.properties" />
```

Place this beneath the line for the import of *compile.xml*.

Now that this is set up, we need a target that can prepare all the directories and copy the files to the right location, so we can later copy this whole bunch to our FTP server:

```
<target name="3.prepare-deployment" description="Prepare all directories and copy file
to a web folder that later can be uploaded" depends="5.clean">
    <mkdir dir="${project.web.path}${file.separator}static${file.separator}"/>
    <mkdir dir="${project.web.path}${file.separator}static${file.separator}swf" />
    <copy todir="${project.web.path}${file.separator}static${file.separator}swf"
flatten="true">
        <resources>
            <file file="${project.bin.path}${file.separator}${project.output.swf}"/>
        </resources>
    </copy>
    <copy todir="${project.web.path}" flatten="true">
        <fileset dir="${project.template.path}"/>
    </copy>
    <delete dir="${project.template.path}"/>
    <eclipse.refreshLocal resource="${project.name}" depth="infinite" />
</target>
```

Here, we make use of Ant tasks we have not yet talked about: mkdir and copy. mkdir is the equivalent of the command mkdir, which you use from the command line to create empty directories. The only parameter it needs is dir, so we can specify the location of the directory to be created.

The other task is copy, which copies a file, or a collection of files, to a folder or directory. It does so by specifying a todir parameter to set the destination. (By default, files are copied only if the source file is newer than the destination file, or when the destination file does not exist. However, you can explicitly overwrite files with the **overwrite** attribute.)

In this example, we use both a resource (a collection of files) and a file set to specify a file or multiple files. The **flatten** parameter ignores the directory structure of the source and just copies the files over.

Let's make contact with the actual FTP server:

```
<target name="4.upload-to-webserver">
    <input message="Please enter your FTP password:" addproperty="remote.ftp.password"
defaultvalue="password" />
    <!-- upload the files to the new directory -->
    <ftp server="${remote.ftp.server}"
        port="${remote.ftp.port}"
        remotedir="${remote.ftp.dir}${file.separator}clients${file.separator}$
{project.name}"
        userid="${remote.ftp.username}"
        password="${remote.ftp.password}"
        verbose="${remote.ftp.verbose}"
        depends="${remote.ftp.depends}"
        binary="${remote.ftp.binary}"
        passive="${remote.ftp.passivemode}">
        <fileset dir="${project.web.path}" />
    </ftp>
    <growl message="Directory ${project.web.path} copied to FTP server
${remote.ftp.server}" />
    <growl message="FTP Transfer Complete." />
</target>
```

We will not yet run this, but when we do, you will notice that Ant provides us with a dialog box where we can input our password. The big plus here is that when we distribute our build files to another team member or share them online, we are not giving away our password. If you don't care about this, you can adjust the property file so the password value is hardcoded.

The final target we will create binds everything together. The problem we have now is that we are calling a target located in a different build file. Step 1 of solving this problem was including the build file in our *depoy.xml* and setting the **as** parameter to a name that suits us. Step 2 of the solution is creating the actual target that calls these imported targets, in the format *as_name_defined_in_import.targetname*.

That target looks like this:

```
<target name="6.test-in-browser" depends="compile.compile, 1.generate-html-template,
3.prepare-deployment, 4.upload-to-webserver">
    <fdt.viewDocument location="${remote.http.server}clients${file.separator}$
{project.name}${file.separator}index.html"/>
</target>
```

This target uses the **depends** parameter to call targets. These need to be completed before Ant can move on. Then it opens a browser with the generated HTML file with the correct SWF file.

By default, this FDT Ant task echoes the location of the URL to open, which will be something like *http://www.my-web-server.com/clients/sample/index.html*.

Here is the complete output of running this target (I'm showing you this so you can see, among other things, what it looks like to load targets from different files):

```
Buildfile: /Personal/O'Reilly/Tools/workspace/sample/deploy.xml

build.create-timestamp:

compile.compile:
        [java] Loading configuration file /SDK/flex_sdk_4.5.0.18623/frameworks/flex-
config.xml
        [java] /Personal/O'Reilly/Tools/workspace/sample/bin/Main_14_08_2011_19_13.swf
(744 bytes)

generate-html-template:

replace-token:

clean:
        [delete] Deleting directory /Personal/O'Reilly/Tools/workspace/sample/web

prepare-deployment:
        [mkdir] Created dir: /Personal/O'Reilly/Tools/workspace/sample/web/static
        [mkdir] Created dir: /Personal/O'Reilly/Tools/workspace/sample/web/static/swf
         [copy] Copying 1 file to /Personal/O'Reilly/Tools/workspace/sample/web/static/
swf
         [copy] Copying 1 file to /Personal/O'Reilly/Tools/workspace/sample/web
        [delete] Deleting directory /Personal/O'Reilly/Tools/workspace/sample/template

upload-to-webserver:
          [ftp] sending files
          [ftp] transferring /Personal/O'Reilly/Tools/workspace/sample/web/index.html
          [ftp] transferring /Personal/O'Reilly/Tools/workspace/sample/web/static/swf/
Main_14_08_2011_19_13.swf
          [ftp] 2 files sent

test-in-browser:
[fdt.viewDocument] open document http://www.myserver.com/clients/sample/index.html
BUILD SUCCESSFUL
Total time: 6 seconds
```

Now that you have all of this finished, you should be proud of yourself! We have learned so much—all about new tasks (`mkdir`, `copy`, `delete`, `input`), token replacement, writing to files, and importing different build files.

Take some time to make yourself a nice cup of coffee or tea and walk around a bit. When you get back, we will continue with deploying to a network share and backing up and zipping the complete project.

Deploying to a Network Share

I've worked at loads of companies where the services department/desk handles your deployments to development or production servers.

The process works like this: you zip your deployment materials, including all your assets (SWF, XML, etc.), copy the zip file over to a network share, and send an email to one of the system or network administrators, who then receives the email in a ticketing system and handles the deployment. So many tedious steps for something that should be so simple. Sound familiar?

With Ant, you can automate even this process.

Let's start with copying everything we want to a directory and cleaning out all the files we don't want. We already used the `copy` and `mkdir` tasks, but the `fileset` and `exclude` tasks are new ones.

`fileset` creates a set from any given directory; and with `include` or `exclude`, you can choose the files you want to select or not select. For example:

```
<target name="7.cleanup-and-export" depends="6.test-in-browser">
    <mkdir dir="${project.deploy.path}" />
    <mkdir dir="${project.zip.path}" />
    <copy overwrite="true" todir="${project.zip.path}">
        <fileset dir="${project.web.path}/">
            <exclude name="**/.settings/**" />
            <exclude name="**/*.as3_classpath" />
            <exclude name="**/*.project" />
            <exclude name="**/.svn/**" />
        </fileset>
    </copy>
    <eclipse.refreshLocal resource="${project.name}" depth="infinite" />
</target>
```

To summarize, we create directories if we don't have them yet, select files we want from a different directory, and filter out the files we don't want to use, so we have only the files we want to include in our zip.

Creating a Zip File

Now that we have all the files we want copied over in a directory, we want to zip the contents of that folder. I prefer zip over different compression file formats, mainly because it does not matter if you are on a Windows, Mac, or *Nix machine. Users in production environments, as well as home users that you need to send zip files to, can uncompress them.

As you can see, a lot of Ant tasks use the same nested elements, like `fileset`. If you wanted to merge multiple zip files in one archive, you would have to use `zipgroupfileset`.

Finally, we clean up the temp folders by using the delete task, and then refresh the workspace to see the changes:

```
<target name="8.create-deployment-zip" description="Create a zip file"
depends="7.cleanup-and-export">
    <zip file="${project.deploy.path}${file.separator}${project.name}_$
{current.date.time}.zip">
        <fileset dir="${project.zip.path}/">
            <include name="**/*" />
        </fileset>
    </zip>
    <!-- create a property to store zip file name in -->
    <property
        name="deployment.zip.file"
        value="${project.deploy.path}${file.separator}${project.name}_
${current.date.time}.zip"/>
    <!-- delete the deploy files from the file system -->
    <delete dir="${project.zip.path}/" />
    <eclipse.refreshLocal resource="${project.name}" depth="infinite" />
</target>
```

As you might have noticed, we also create a property for the name of our zip file, so we can use it later in the chained-up process by calling **${deployment.zip.file}**.

We have now gone through all the steps for creating a deployment, zipping it up, and generating files. Next, we need to copy the files to a network share.

Let's add some properties to the *remote.properties* file:

```
# Local network share properties
share.project=/Volumes/Deployments/
share.project.dir=${project.name}/
```

As for the actual target, you can see it is no different from doing a normal file copy, since we have the network drive mounted to our system and defined the path in the *remote.properties* file:

```
<target name="9.copy-to-networkshare" depends="8.create-deployment-zip">
    <growl message="Copying file with name: ${deployment.zip.file}"/>
    <growl message="To the this location:   ${share.project}${share.project.dir}"/>
    <copy
        todir="${share.project}${share.project.dir}"
        file="${deployment.zip.file}" />
</target>
```

Making a Backup of the Complete Project

Instead of making a zip file from only one directory, we create a backup of the complete project. So, besides using SVN and not losing your code, we create a failsafe and back up all our files (this zip file can later be committed to SVN, too, of course):

```
<target name="10.create-backup-zip" description="Create a zip file that holds all the
project files" depends="build.create-timestamp">
    <zip file="${project.backup.path}${file.separator}backup_${project.name}_$
```

```
{current.date.time}.zip">
        <fileset dir="${basedir}/">
            <include name="**/*" />
            <exclude name="**/.settings/**" />
            <exclude name="**/*.as3_classpath" />
            <exclude name="**/*.project" />
            <exclude name="**/.svn/**" />
        </fileset>
    </zip>
    <eclipse.refreshLocal resource="${project.name}" depth="infinite" />
</target>
```

We exclude a lot of hidden files (settings and other miscellaneous files—stuff we can do without); we only want a backup of the complete project.

The *build.properties* file also needs to be adjusted slightly. The following is only the project properties defined; the rest, we can leave alone:

```
# Project Properties
project.name=sample
project.document.class=Main
project.file.extension=.as
project.src.path=${basedir}${file.separator}src
project.bin.path=${basedir}${file.separator}bin
project.template.path=${basedir}${file.separator}template
project.debug.path=${basedir}${file.separator}debug
project.deploy.path=${basedir}${file.separator}deploy
project.assets.path=${basedir}${file.separator}assets
project.web.path=${basedir}${file.separator}web
project.zip.path=${basedir}${file.separator}zip
project.backup.path=${basedir}${file.separator}backup
project.classpath=${project.src.path}${file.separator}com${file.separator}sample$
{file.separator}
```

We saved the best for last. Now it's time to send that email (the one that goes to the support desk and one to yourself).

Emailing the Client/Support Desk

Why is emailing useful? We already discussed this a little bit at the beginning of this chapter. Let's say you have three responsibilities: deploying via the service desk, updating your project manager about what is left to do, and keeping your team informed about the project's status.

You have several different options available when you send an email: plain text, different encodings, with or without attachments, and more. Ant can handle all of the above, and we will go through each of your aforementioned responsibilities to show you how.

We can, of course, send an email to three people every time we do a deployment. But what if you deploy every hour, or even every half hour? Doing this task by hand—over and over again—is tedious, to say the least!

So we won't. Let's hand over this task to Ant and let it deal with it. Much easier, right? What do we need?

- One email with the deployment assets to the service desk
- One email to the project manager
- One email to your team

Let's take a step back. Normally when you write code, you place your //TODO and //FIXME notes all over the place, mostly for your own reference and so your team knows what is happening and what still needs to be fixed.

Now wouldn't it be nice if we could have an Ant task to read through all our class files, get our //TODOs, place them in a file, and mail them to you, or to someone else so that person could see what was left to do?

Luckily for us, a developer, Alex Collins from England, has already created such a project: Ant TODO. Alex and I have been in contact to make these tasks even more useful. He has also implemented some new features, like saving the output to a property so you can reuse it in different targets, and outputting and supporting both TODO and FIXME.

 You can find out more about Alex Collins—enterprise Java developer by day; Linux, Android, and Python open source hacker by night—on his website, *http://alexcollins.org/*, and at *http://madalex.net/*.

For more information about the Ant TODO project, downloads, and source files, go to *http://code.google.com/p/ant-todo/*.

So let's begin with installing Ant TODO and then we'll set up the actual emailing.

If you download the *ant-todo*.jar* from Google Code, you have the latest version. I have also included this JAR file in the zip file, so it should already be in your classpath. If it is not, open up Eclipse's preferences and go to the Ant section. Then select Runtime. Here, you have to add an external JAR file to the Global Entries section. Don't forget to click Apply to set the changes. Sometimes it is better to restart Eclipse for the changes to take effect.

Open up Eclipse and open the *build.xml* file. We need to make sure the classes at the top of this file are imported so we can use them throughout the project:

```
<!-- Import Growl Classes so we can send notifications via Growl -->
<taskdef name="growl" classname="net.slimeslurp.growl.GrowlEcho" />

<!-- Import TODOTask so we can get out all //TODO: //FIXME: from src folder. -->
<taskdef name="todo" classname="org.atc.tools.ant.TODOTask" />
```

Then go to *deploy.xml* and create a new target called make-todo-list.

There are a couple of options available when you're using this library. You can write output to a file using CVS, XML, or plain-text format by setting the `format=` parameter to `cvs`, `xml`, or `default`, respectively. If you omit this parameter, it defaults to plain text.

For now, we want to write to a file in plain text:

```
<target name="make-todo-list">
    <todo dir="src" format="default" outFile="todo-list.txt" verbose="true" />
</target>
```

The `verbose` parameter gives you additional information while parsing all your files.

When we open the file, we see output similar to this:

```
Main.as[linenumber]: Init App utils for loader objects and flashvars
Main.as[linenumber]: Add contextMenu with information
Version.as[linenumber]: Do specific development stuff here
Version.as[linenumber]: Do specific production stuff here
ApplicationUtils.as[linenumber]: Is regex good here?
ApplicationUtils.as[linenumber]: just testing my todo items
```

As you can see, it shows you the class name, line number, and the comment after the `//TODO:`, and every item is on a new line.

We can also output to a property so we can reuse it in different targets:

```
<target name="make-todo-list">
    <todo dir="src" property="todo.list" verbose="true" />
</target>
```

Or do both (write to file and use as a property):

```
<target name="make-todo-list">
    <todo dir="src" property="todo.list"
        format="default" outFile="todo-list.txt"  verbose="true" />
</target>
```

We can also set different file filters. In the preceding examples, we included all files, regardless of their file extension. But we could also set these only to *.as* class files, like so:

```
<target name="make-todo-list">
    <todo dir="src" property="todo.list" verbose="true" />
        <include name="**/*.as" />
    </todo>
</target>
```

You can even set the `pattern=` and `replace=` properties to replace pieces of the output string:

```
<target name="make-todo-list">
    <todo dir="src" property="todo.list"
        pattern="[A-Za-z]" replace="*"/>
        <include name="**/*.as" />
    </todo>
</target>
```

This replaces all the uppercase and lowercase characters with a star—not very useful, but you can adjust the regular expression value with anything you want.

And then, later on, we can call the newly created ${todo.list} property to output this complete list. In the sample project, I have also placed some Java files so you can see the difference in the file filters.

The complete sample project for this book, with all the code and every example, can be found at *http://book.funky-monkey.nl/*.

We have our to-do list sorted, so let's move on to emailing and the different options.

Before we can start to send email to people, we need to have some external libraries; the ability to send email is not built into Ant by default.

I have provided those libs in the book's zip files, which you can download from *http://book.funky-monkey.nl/* in the *ready_to_import* folder.

Sun also provides the necessary downloads—the JavaMail API and the JavaBeans Activation Framework—on its website at the following locations: *http://www.oracle.com/technetwork/java/index-138643.html* and *http://www.oracle.com/technetwork/java/javase/downloads/index-135046.html*.

Just unpack them, put them in the location where the rest of the Ant JAR files for this book's exercises live, and add them to the Eclipse Ant classpath.

Sending email in its most basic form is very easy: call the mail task and provide a "to" address, a "from" address, and a subject:

```
<mail from="me" tolist="you" subject="A mail from Ant" />
```

It would be nice if we could add an extra piece of information regarding the email sent, so we need some user input. We have done this before, remember? We need an input task. We'll start by taking the user's additional message and save it to a property:

```
<target name="11.email-with-attachment-and-todo" depends="make-todo-list, 8.create-
deployment-zip">
    <input message="Add an additional message to the deployment or service desk."
addproperty="email.deployment.service.message" />
```

This target depends on the creation of a new compilation, an upload to your FTP server, and eventually the creation of a zip file. This zip file is then placed in the *deploy* directory and attached to our email to the service desk:

```
<mail mailhost="smtp.euronet.nl" mailport="25" subject="Deployment">
    <from address="me_email@euronet.nl"/>
    <replyto address="me_email@euronet.nl"/>
```

```
        <to address="my_emailadres@my-server.com"/>
            <message>Hello,
Can you deploy this file to the staging server on:
${remote.http.server}

Please note the following:

${email.deployment.service.message}

Kind regards,
${user.name}</message>
            <attachments>
                <fileset dir="${project.deploy.path}">
                    <include name="**/*.zip"/>
                </fileset>
            </attachments>
        </mail>
```

Note that I deliberately formatted the message between the <message> tags in this way because this is also the format in which the mail will be received.

But we're not quite there yet. We still need to send a mail to our project manager and to our team.

Again, we want an extra message to be sent alongside the email to our project manager. So, again, we need to store the additional message in a property when the user has given us input:

```
<input message="Add an additional message to project mananger"
addproperty="email.pm.message" />
    <mail mailhost="smtp.euronet.nl" mailport="25" subject="Open TODO items">
    <from address="me_email@euronet.nl"/>
    <replyto address="me_email@euronet.nl"/>
    <to address="my_emailaddress@my-server.com"/>
    <message>Hello Mr. Project Mananger,
This is my open TODO list for today:

${todo.list}

Please note the following:

${email.pm.message}

Kind regards,
${user.name}</message>
    </mail>
```

The last email goes to our team. The **tolist** parameter takes a comma-separated list of email addresses, so we can specify more than one team member:

```
<mail mailhost="smtp.euronet.nl" mailport="25" subject="Dont forget!" tolist="
you@email.com, you@email.com">
    <from address="me_email@euronet.nl"/>
    <replyto address="me_email@euronet.nl"/>
    <message>Hi team,
Don't forget, this list is still open todo:
```

```
${todo.list}

Kind regards,
${user.name}</message>
</mail>
```

If you use your own mail server, you can also provide the SMTP host with a username and password. So, there you have it: three different options for sending mail with Ant (Figure 3-16).

Of course, you can save this recipients list in a property. As an independent exercise, add a new file called *email.properties*, list a bunch of email addresses there, and include that in your newly created target. After doing this, you can take out the input field.

me_email		**Dont forget!** - Hi team, Don't forget, this list is still open
me_email		**Open TODO items** - Hello Mr. Project Mananger, This is
me_email		**Deployment** - Hello, Can you deploy this file the staging

Figure 3-16. Sending multiple emails with Ant

Adobe AIR and Mobile Compiling

Aside from normal compiling, we can also compile to AIR (Adobe Integrated Runtime) and to mobile platforms like Android and iOS.

Let's start off with compiling for AIR. AIR gives you the ability to create "Flash outside of the browser" applications or desktop applications. The cool thing about AIR is that if you create your application once, with AS3, you can use the same codebase to export to SWF, the desktop, Android, and iOS, with only some minor adjustments to the application descriptor file.

If you want to start developing with AIR, you need the AIR SDK. The latest public release at the time of this writing is the AIR 2.7 SDK, which can be found at *http://www.adobe.com/products/air/sdk/*.

This SDK also includes the ADL (AIR Debug Launcher) and ADT (AIR Developer Tool) command-line tools. We will be using this SDK in our examples.

After you have downloaded the AIR SDK, it is time to overlay it with the Flex SDK we downloaded earlier. This is a relatively painless process if you know what to do. Be sure to make a backup of your Flex SDK folder before starting. Better safe than sorry!

Copy the downloaded SDK file to the location where you extracted the Flex SDK. I have a folder on the root of my machine called *SDK* where I place all my SDKs.

On Windows, just right-click the zip file (the AIR SDK) in the Flex SDK folder and select Extract All or use any decompression tool of your choice.

Mac OS X is a bit different. When you extract the SDK here, it's possible that it won't copy the correct file permissions, so you are stuck with something that does not work.

To make it work, we open up Terminal and go to the directory of the Flex SDK. Type **cd** followed by a space. Now you can drag the path of the Flex SDK from the Finder to your Terminal app to copy the path. (Depending on where your SDK folder lives, I've found this method to be faster than cd'ing to that directory.)

Then, type the following command in Terminal:

```
tar jxvf AdobeAIRSDK.tbz2
```

If you have permission problems or ADL returns a message saying "error=13, Permission denied" when compiling, then try:

```
sudo tar jxvf AdobeAIRSDK.tbz2
```

This makes sure that all the file permissions are correct and we don't have any problems. If you still have the problems, try overlaying the AIR SDK again.

If you see filenames and filepaths flying past on your screen, don't worry; this is the extraction process. After this operation, the Flex SDK will be merged with the AIR SDK.

Compiling and Packaging to AIR

AIR works a little differently than a normal AS3 project. It works with XML application descriptor files that hold specific information about the application. These files have a naming convention of *NameOfProject-app.xml*.

A sample descriptor file looks like this:

```
<?xml version="1.0" encoding="utf-8" ?>
<application xmlns="http://ns.adobe.com/air/application/2.7">
    <id>com.sample.Main</id>
    <name>My Funky App</name>
    <filename>MyFunkyApp</filename>
    <versionNumber>1.0.0</versionNumber>
    <copyright>Copyright (c) 2011 Sidney de Koning</copyright>
    <installFolder>Adobe Air/MyFunkyApp</installFolder>
    <programMenuFolder></programMenuFolder>

    <description>
        <text xml:lang="en">Here comes my install description</text>
    </description>

    <supportedProfiles>desktop</supportedProfiles>

    <initialWindow>
        <title>MyFunkyApp</title>
        <content>Main.swf</content>
        <transparent>false</transparent>
```

```
            <visible>true</visible>
            <minimizable>true</minimizable>
            <maximizable>false</maximizable>
            <resizable>true</resizable>
            <renderMode>auto</renderMode>
            <width>480</width>
            <height>800</height>
            <minSize>480 800</minSize>
            <maxSize>1280 960</maxSize>
        </initialWindow>

        <icon>
            <image16x16>assets/icons/AIRApp_16.png</image16x16>
            <image32x32>assets/icons/AIRApp_32.png</image32x32>
            <image48x48>assets/icons/AIRApp_48.png</image48x48>
            <image128x128>assets/icons/AIRApp_128.png</image128x128>
        </icon>

        <customUpdateUI>false</customUpdateUI>
        <allowBrowserInvocation>false</allowBrowserInvocation>
        <fileTypes>
            <fileType>
                <name>adobe.VideoFile</name>
                <extension>avf</extension>
                <description>Adobe Video File</description>
                <contentType>application/vnd.adobe.video-file</contentType>

                <icon>
                    <image16x16>icons/AIRApp_16.png</image16x16>
                    <image32x32>icons/AIRApp_32.png</image32x32>
                    <image48x48>icons/AIRApp_48.png</image48x48>
                    <image128x128>icons/AIRApp_128.png</image128x128>
                </icon>
            </fileType>
        </fileTypes>
    </application>
```

AIR needs this information to package to an actual *.air* file, which is basically a zip file with no compression that holds all your packaged assets, XML files, and the compiled SWF (kind of like the JAR file we've already talked about).

 Please note that the format of this descriptor file tends to change a lot; it's not set in stone. Be sure to look for changes when a new version of the AIR SDK comes out.

To compile to AIR, you compile like you normally would, only you add one parameter to the compilation, `configname=air`, and you set the SWF version with `swf-version=12`. This forces the compiler to spit out the correct SWF version. We'll come back to this later.

We will write three targets: one to create a certificate, one to compile, and one to package. Let's see if you can create the debugging target yourself.

First, open up the *sdk.properties* file and add the following line. This will allow us to call the ADT and pass a parameter to it:

```
sdk.adt.compiler=${sdk.location}${file.separator}lib${file.separator}adt.jar
```

We also need a reference to ADL. Note that unlike all the other files Adobe provides in JAR format, ADL is platform-dependent, which is a shame because now not everything is cross-platform. You can, of course, solve this with Ant's env property and choose either adl or adl.exe, depending on which OS you are on.

For now, we will keep it in one property. Feel free to make this truly cross-platform, however:

```
# This is the only platform-specific file. For Window this needs to be adl.exe
sdk.adl.compiler=${sdk.location}${file.separator}bin${file.separator}adl
```

The certificate we will create will be *self-signed*, which means that there is no certificate authority behind it. The difference between this and a purchased certificate is that when you publish to AIR on the desktop, you will see a "publisher could not be verified" dialog.

Having a certificate from an authority does not matter for your app's inner workings, but it could help you when you want to distribute your AIR apps. Alarm bells will start ringing when your user sees software from an unknown source and a message displaying a big red cross. Besides, it looks nicer to have your own certificate (Figure 3-17).

Figure 3-17. Using your signed certificate from a certificate authority

Creating a Self-Signed Certificate

Now that we have all the properties set, we can start with the target creation. But how do we know what to create or call the ADL?

Adobe has very good documentation online. If you search the Live Docs for "Creating a self-signed certificate with ADT," you will find that the command to feed ADT directly is as follows:

```
adt -certificate -cn name -ou org-unit -o org-name -c country -validityPeriod years
(key_type 1024-RSA | 2048-RSA) pfx-file password
```

 The Live Docs URL for command-line tools is *http://livedocs.adobe.com/ flex/3/html/help.html?content=CommandLineTools_6.html.*

This command looks pretty straightforward, and it translates directly to our properties.

Create a new property file called *cert.properties* in the *ant* folder. This is where we'll store all the properties needed for our certificate:

```
# Certificate Properties used for AIR and Android
certificate.name=myTestCert
certificate.password=myPass1234;
certificate.extension=pfx
certificate.validity.years=30
certificate.organization.name=My Fake Organization
certificate.organization.unit=Mobile Dev
certificate.organization.country=NL
certificate.organization.keystrength=2048-RSA
certificate.location.path=${basedir}${file.separator}certificate
```

If we look at the ADT command, we can very easily create a target from that information:

```
<target name="air-create-new-certificate">
    <mkdir dir="${certificate.location.path}" />
    <java jar="${sdk.adt.compiler}" fork="true"
        failonerror="true" logError="true">
        <arg value="-certificate" />
        <arg value="-cn" />
        <arg value="${certificate.name}" />
        <arg value="-ou" />
        <arg value="${certificate.organization.unit}" />
        <arg value="-o" />
        <arg value="${certificate.organization.name}" />
        <arg value="-c" />
        <arg value="${certificate.organization.country}" />
        <arg value="${certificate.organization.keystrength}" />
        <arg value="${certificate.location.path}${file.separator}${certificate.name}.
${certificate.extension}" />
        <arg value="${certificate.password}" />
    </java>
    <growl message="Created self signed certificate" />
    <eclipse.refreshLocal resource="${project.name}" depth="infinite" />
</target>
```

This creates a new certificate called *myTestCert.pfx* in the *certificate* directory. That was easy, right? Let's move on to something a little harder: compiling to AIR.

Remember the compile target from the mxmlc compiling? Let's refresh a bit. It looked like this:

```
<target name="compile" description="Compile a SWF with MXMLC Compiler"
depends="build.create-timestamp">
    <java jar="${sdk.mxmlc.compiler}" fork="true" failonerror="true">
        <arg value="-debug=false" />
        <arg value="-optimize=true" />
        <arg value="-verbose-stacktraces=true" />
        <arg value="+flexlib=${sdk.libs.framework}" />
        <arg value="-source-path=${project.src.path}" />
        <arg value="-library-path=${sdk.libs.location}" />
        <arg value="-file-specs=${project.classpath}${project.document.class}
${project.file.extension}" />
        <arg value="-output=${project.bin.path}${file.separator}
${project.document.class}_${current.date.time}.swf" />
    </java>
    <property name="project.output.swf"
value="${project.document.class}_${current.date.time}.swf"/>
    <eclipse.refreshLocal resource="${project.name}" depth="infinite" />
</target>
```

As I said earlier, we only need to add the configname=air and the swf-version=12 to the compilation parameter. Let's create a target for specific AIR compiling. What we're actually doing is creating a SWF that is suitable and prepared for AIR packaging.

So we will take the old code and adjust it to:

```
<target name="compile-to-air" description="Compile a SWF for AIR use"
depends="build.create-timestamp, make-dirs">
    <java jar="${sdk.mxmlc.compiler}" fork="true" failonerror="true">
        <arg value="-debug=false" />
        <arg value="-optimize=true" />
        <arg value="+configname=air" />
        <arg value="-swf-version=12" />
        <arg value="-verbose-stacktraces=true" />
        <arg value="+flexlib=${sdk.libs.framework}" />
        <arg value="-source-path=${project.src.path}" />
        <arg value="-library-path=${sdk.libs.location}" />
        <arg value="-file-specs=${project.classpath}
${project.document.class}${project.file.extension}" />
        <arg value="-output=${project.build.path}${file.separator}
${project.document.class}.swf" />
    </java>
    <property name="project.output.swf" value="${project.document.class}.swf"/>
    <growl message="Compiling SWF for AIR completed." />
    <eclipse.refreshLocal resource="${project.name}" depth="infinite" />
</target>
```

As you can see, we removed the date in the filename because we don't need it for now. Since we remove the directories we build to, everything is cleaned up so we have a new

SWF every time. For this compilation process, we need two more targets and some new properties.

Create a new file called *air.properties* and add this:

```
# AIR and AIR for Android Properties
air.app.name=MyFunkyApp
air.app.descriptor.path=${basedir}${file.separator}descriptor
air.app.descriptor=${air.app.descriptor.path}${file.separator}${air.app.name}-app.xml
air.app.file=${air.app.name}.air
```

And to the *build.properties*, add:

```
project.build.path=${basedir}${file.separator}build
project.publish.path=${basedir}${file.separator}publish
```

This target depends on a `make-dirs`, which in turn depends on a `clean`, just like before. Here's the target for cleaning:

```
<target name="clean">
    <delete dir="${project.build.path}" />
    <delete dir="${project.publish.path}" />
    <eclipse.refreshLocal resource="${project.name}" depth="infinite" />
</target>
```

and here's the target for making directories:

```
<target name="make-dirs" depends="clean">
    <mkdir dir="${project.build.path}" />
    <mkdir dir="${project.publish.path}" />
    <eclipse.refreshLocal resource="${project.name}" depth="infinite" />
</target>
```

What we end up with is a SWF file that is ready to be packaged into an *.air* file. First, we want to test whether everything went OK with the compilation; we'll do so by calling the ADL to test our file.

The command in ADL is as follows:

```
adl [-runtime runtime-directory] [-pubid publisher-id] [-nodebug] application.xml
[root-directory] [-- arguments]
```

The only thing we need to provide is the application descriptor XML and the build path to find the SWF:

```
<target name="air-test-app" depends="compile-to-air">
    <exec executable="${sdk.adl.compiler}">
        <arg value="${air.app.descriptor}" />
        <arg value="${project.build.path}" />
    </exec>
    <growl message="Testing Application in AIR (Desktop)." />
</target>
```

This opens ADL and shows us our SWF wrapped in AIR. Congrats! But we are not quite there yet.

Now we need to package the application and sign it with our self-signed certificate. Again, we look up the command for ADT:

```
adt -package -storetype type -keystore store -storepass pass -target air output-
package app-descriptor -C dir fileOrDir input-package
```

And again we can easily translate this to an Ant target:

```
<target name="pakage-to-air" depends="compile-to-air">
    <java jar="${sdk.adt.compiler}" fork="true" failonerror="true">
        <arg value="-package" />
        <arg value="-storetype" />
        <arg value="pkcs12" />
        <arg value="-keystore" />
        <arg value="${certificate.location.path}${file.separator}${certificate.name}.
${certificate.extension}" />
        <arg value="-storepass" />
        <arg value="${certificate.password}" />
        <arg value="${project.publish.path}/${air.app.file}" />
        <arg value="${air.app.descriptor}" />
        <arg value="-C" />
        <arg value="${project.build.path}" />
        <arg value="${project.output.swf}" />
        <arg value="-C" />
        <arg value="${project.assets.path}" />
        <arg value="icons" />
    </java>
    <growl message="Packaging AIR Application completed." />
    <eclipse.refreshLocal resource="${project.name}" depth="infinite" />
</target>
```

Now give yourself a well-deserved pat on the back. You have just created, compiled, packaged, and signed your first AIR application for the desktop with Ant. You can be very proud of yourself!

Compiling and Packaging to an Android APK

As of version 2.7 of the AIR SDK, there is no need to download the Android SDK if you want to compile to an Android APK file. Everything you need is packaged in the AIR SDK itself, even the device and emulator runtime APK files.

That is good news and means we can use ADT for the compilation. We just need to find out the commands to do so.

The only reason we need the Android SDK is for logging to LogCat, the integrated Android logger for Eclipse, or if we don't have an actual device to debug in the emulator.

Compiling to Android APK

To create the AIR package for Android that outputs an APK file, use the following command:

```
adt -package -target (apk | apk-debug | apk-emulator | apk-profile) -storetype pkcs12
-keystore sampleCert.p12 MyApp.apk MyApp-app.xml MyApp.swf icons/128x128Icon.png
icons/48x48icon.png icons/32x32icon.png icons/16x16icon.png
```

As you can see, we have different package options. For now, we only want to use the apk option in our Ant target. If you want to debug, you can use apk-debug, but you will also need a SWF that is compiled with the debug=true flag.

Here are the Android package targets, according to the Adobe.com Live Docs:

apk

> An Android package. A package produced with this target can only be installed on an Android device, not an emulator.

apk-debug

> An Android package with extra debugging information. (The SWF files in the application must also be compiled with debugging support.)

apk-emulator

> An Android package for use on an emulator without debugging support. (Use the apk-debug target to permit debugging on both emulators and devices.)

So, again, we can easily create an Ant target with this. We have the groundwork done, so let's begin by adding the properties.

Open up *certificate.properties* and add the extension for a specific Android certificate. This is a different format (p12):

```
certificate.android.extension=p12
```

Then we need to add some properties to *android.properties*. So let's create that and place it in the *ant* folder:

```
# AIR for Android Properties
android.file.extension=apk
android.app.file=${air.app.name}.${android.file.extension}
android.app.descriptor=${air.app.descriptor.path}${file.separator}${air.app.name}-
Android-app.xml
android.app.icon.path=${project.assets.path}${file.separator}icons${file.separator}
```

As you can see from the preceding code, we have to make a slightly different Android descriptor file. The difference lies in the supportedProfiles node and the Android node. Its filename is based on the name ${air.app.name} property and eventually becomes *MyFunkyApp-Android-app.xml*. The contents of this complete file are displayed below.

The manifest addition needs certain permissions to work; on the Android system, the app itself needs to get permission from the system to use certain resources. You can find the complete list of permissions that AIR can use on Adobe's Live Docs site:

```xml
<?xml version="1.0" encoding="utf-8" ?>
<application xmlns="http://ns.adobe.com/air/application/2.7">
    <id>com.sample.Main</id>
    <name>My Funky App</name>
    <filename>MyFunkyApp</filename>
    <versionNumber>1.0.0</versionNumber>
    <copyright>Copyright (c) 2011 Sidney de Koning</copyright>
    <installFolder>Adobe Air/MyFunkyApp</installFolder>
    <programMenuFolder>MyFunkyApp</programMenuFolder>

    <description>
        <text xml:lang="en">Here comes my install description</text>
    </description>

    <supportedProfiles>mobileDevice</supportedProfiles>

    <initialWindow>
        <title>MyFunkyApp</title>
        <content>build/Main.swf</content>
        <transparent>false</transparent>
        <visible>true</visible>
        <minimizable>true</minimizable>
        <maximizable>false</maximizable>
        <resizable>true</resizable>
        <renderMode>auto</renderMode>
        <width>480</width>
        <height>800</height>
        <minSize>480 800</minSize>
        <maxSize>1280 960</maxSize>
        <!-- <width>640</width> <height>480</height> <minSize>320 240</minSize>
            <maxSize>1280 960</maxSize> -->
    </initialWindow>
    <icon>
        <image16x16>assets/icons/AIRApp_16.png</image16x16>
        <image32x32>assets/icons/ATRApp_32.png</image32x32>
        <image48x48>assets/icons/AIRApp_48.png</image48x48>
        <image128x128>assets/icons/AIRApp_128.png</image128x128>
    </icon>
    <customUpdateUI>true</customUpdateUI>
    <allowBrowserInvocation>false</allowBrowserInvocation>
    <android>
        <manifestAdditions>
        <![CDATA[
            <manifest android:installLocation="preferExternal">
                <uses-permission android:name="android.permission.INTERNET" />
            </manifest>
        ]]>
        </manifestAdditions>
    </android>
    <fileTypes>
        <fileType>
            <name>adobe.VideoFile</name>
            <extension>avf</extension>
            <description>Adobe Video File</description>
            <contentType>application/vnd.adobe.video-file</contentType>
```

```
<icon>
    <image16x16>assets/icons/AIRApp_16.png</image16x16>
    <image32x32>assets/icons/AIRApp_32.png</image32x32>
    <image48x48>assets/icons/AIRApp_48.png</image48x48>
    <image128x128>assets/icons/AIRApp_128.png</image128x128>
</icon>
        </fileType>
    </fileTypes>
</application>
```

Now we need to create the *air.xml* build file. We are going to need some properties and some targets. First, we need to include those properties so we can use them:

```
<!-- Import all properties etc. -->
<import file="build.xml" as="build" />
<import file="air.xml" as="air" />
<property file="ant/air.properties" />
<property file="ant/android.properties" />
<property file="ant/certificate.properties" />
```

Then we can move on to the actual targets. Since Android needs a certificate with a different functionality and thus a different extension—the p12 we talked about earlier—we need to create a new target for it to work:

```
<target name="android-create-new-certificate">
    <mkdir dir="${certificate.location.path}" />
    <java jar="${sdk.adt.compiler}" fork="true" failonerror="true" logError="true">
        <arg value="-certificate" />
        <arg value="-cn" />
        <arg value="${certificate.name}" />
        <arg value="-ou" />
        <arg value="${certificate.organization.unit}" />
        <arg value="-o" />
        <arg value="${certificate.organization.name}" />
        <arg value="-c" />
        <arg value="${certificate.organization.country}" />
        <arg value="-validityPeriod" />
        <arg value="${certificate.validity.years}" />
        <arg value="${certificate.organization.keystrength}" />
        <arg value="${project.build.path}${file.separator}${certificate.name}.
${certificate.android.extension}" />
        <arg value="${certificate.password}" />
    </java>
    <growl message="Created a new Self Signed Certificate for Android" />
    <eclipse.refreshLocal resource="${project.name}" depth="infinite" />
</target>
```

If we want to actually compile to a native Android APK file, let's look up the command for it and create it:

```
<target name="pakage-to-apk" depends="air.compile-to-air">
    <java jar="${sdk.adt.compiler}" fork="true" failonerror="true">
        <arg value="-package" />
        <arg value="-target" />
        <arg value="${android.file.extension}" />
```

```
        <arg value="-storetype" />
        <arg value="pkcs12" />
        <arg value="-keystore" />
        <arg value="${certificate.location.path}${file.separator}${certificate.name}.
${certificate.android.extension}" />
        <arg value="-storepass" />
        <arg value="${certificate.password}" />
    <arg value="${project.publish.path}${file.separator}${air.app.name}.
${android.file.extension}" />
        <arg value="${android.app.descriptor}" />
        <arg value="${project.build.path}${file.separator}${project.output.swf}" />
        <arg value="${android.app.icon.path}AIRApp_128.png" />
        <arg value="${android.app.icon.path}AIRApp_48.png" />
        <arg value="${android.app.icon.path}AIRApp_32.png" />
        <arg value="${android.app.icon.path}AIRApp_16.png" />
    </java>
    <growl message="Packaging APK Application completed." />
    <eclipse.refreshLocal resource="${project.name}" depth="infinite" />
</target>
```

This is nothing we haven't done before. You have to make sure to enter the commands in the right order; otherwise, you will get errors. Some common problems that can occur are that the location of the SWF in the descriptor file is incorrect or the icons are not packaged along with the APK.

That is all there is to compiling and packaging for Android. Let's see if you can create your own targets for debugging and installing the APK file on your phone or to the emulator based on the command in the beginning of this chapter.

If you want to test your own apps on your Android phone, you have to make sure you can install apps from sources other than the Android Market. How? It's easy: click the menu button on your home screen and then choose Settings→Applications→Unknown sources.

Compiling for iOS

Wouldn't it be great if we could target iOS as well? (That means iPhone/iPod and iPad.)

Let's create an *ios.properties* file in the *ant* folder and add the following:

```
# iOS Properties
ios.file.extension=ipa
ios.app.file=${air.app.name}.${ios.file.extension}
ios.app.descriptor=${air.app.descriptor.path}${file.separator}${air.app.name}-iOS-
app.xml
```

Personally, I have found it more convenient to work with separate descriptor files. The iOS version of our descriptor also needs slightly different information and has different icon sizes.

You can make the distinction to develop only for iPad or only for iPhone/iPod by changing the UIDeviceFamily string to either 1 or 2. You can use both nodes to target both. A value of 1 means iPhone/iPod; 2 means only iPad. In the following example, right now we are targeting both iPad and iPhone/iPod:

```
<key>UIDeviceFamily</key>
    <array>
        <string>1</string>
        <string>2</string>
    </array>
```

The descriptor file has some minor adjustments from the previous descriptor files we talked about—mostly the icons and the iPhone tag inside the XML:

```xml
<?xml version="1.0" encoding="utf-8" ?>
<application xmlns="http://ns.adobe.com/air/application/2.7">
    <id>com.sample.Main</id>
    <name>My Funky App</name>
    <filename>MyFunkyApp</filename>
    <versionNumber>1.0.0</versionNumber>
    <copyright>Copyright (c) 2011 Sidney de Koning</copyright>
    <installFolder>Adobe Air/MyFunkyApp</installFolder>

    <description>
        <text xml:lang="en">Here comes my install description</text>
    </description>

    <supportedProfiles>mobileDevice</supportedProfiles>

    <initialWindow>
        <title>MyFunkyApp</title>
        <content>build/Main.swf</content>
        <transparent>false</transparent>
        <visible>true</visible>
        <minimizable>true</minimizable>
        <maximizable>false</maximizable>
        <resizable>true</resizable>
        <renderMode>auto</renderMode>
        <width>480</width>
        <height>800</height>
        <minSize>480 800</minSize>
        <maxSize>1280 960</maxSize>
        <!-- <width>640</width> <height>480</height> <minSize>320 240</minSize>
            <maxSize>1280 960</maxSize> -->
    </initialWindow>
    <icon>
        <image29x29>assets/icons/iOSicon-29.png</image29x29>
        <image57x57>assets/icons/iOSicon-57.png</image57x57>
        <image512x512>assets/icons/iOSicon-512.png</image512x512>
    </icon>

    <iPhone>
        <InfoAdditions>
        <![CDATA[
            <key>UIDeviceFamily</key>
            <array>
                <string>1</string>
            </array>
```

```
            <key>UIRequiresPersistentWiFi</key>
            <string>NO</string>
            <key>UIApplicationExitsOnSuspend</key>
            <string>YES</string>
        ]]>
        </InfoAdditions>
    </iPhone>
    <customUpdateUI>true</customUpdateUI>
    <allowBrowserInvocation>false</allowBrowserInvocation>
</application>
```

Certificates for iOS

Certificates on iOS work a little differently from those we are accustomed to for AIR
and Android. Developing for iOS requires you to buy certificates from Apple. At the
time of this writing, the price of a certificate is $99. The creation of this certificate and
provisioning file is beyond the scope of this book, but there are loads of resources online
that can help you with this. We are sticking to only the topic of compiling to an iOS
native format.

 For more information on certificates and how to create them, go to *http:*
//developer.apple.com/devcenter/ios/index.action.

For demonstration purposes, let's assume you already have a certificate. Next, we add
the location and password to our *certificate.properties* file:

```
# iOS Certificate locations
certificate.ios.provisioning.file.path=/Certificaten/development/
myProvisioning.mobileprovision
certificate.ios.cert.file.path=/Certificaten/development/development_flash_iphone.p12
certificate.ios.password=myPassword
ios.app.icon.path=${project.assets.path}${file.separator}icons${file.separator}
```

The following is the command for compiling to iOS (it does not differ much from how
we called ADT before when packaging to APK):

```
adt -package -target ( ipa-test | ipa-debug | ipa-app-store | ipa-ad-hoc | ipa-test-
interpreter | ipa-debug-interpreter ) CONNECT_OPTIONS? SIGNING_OPTIONS <output-
package> ( FILE_OPTIONS | <input-package> )
```

As you can see, you have a lot of options: `ipa-test`, `ipa-debug`, `ipa-app-store`, `ipa-ad-
hoc`, `ipa-test-interpreter`, and `ipa-debug-interpreter`. The following is a list of all the
package targets you have for iOS, according to Adobe's Live Docs:

`ipa-ad-hoc`
An iOS package for ad hoc distribution.

`ipa-app-store`
An iOS package for Apple App Store distribution.

ipa-debug
> An iOS package with extra debugging information. (The SWF files in the application must also be compiled with debugging support.)

ipa-test
> An iOS package compiled without optimization or debugging information.

ipa-debug-interpreter
> Functionally equivalent to a debug package, but compiles more quickly. However, the ActionScript bytecode is interpreted and not translated to machine code. As a result, code execution is slower in an interpreter package.

ipa-test-interpreter
> Functionally equivalent to a test package, but compiles more quickly. However, the ActionScript bytecode is interpreted and not translated to machine code. As a result, code execution is slower in an interpreter package.

For now, the only ones we need are ipa-debug and, if you want to distribute to the App Store, ipa-app-store. The target will be:

```
<target name="package-to-ios" depends="air.compile-to-air">
    <java jar="${sdk.adt.compiler}" fork="true" failonerror="true">
        <arg line="-package" />
        <arg line="-target" />
        <arg line="ipa-debug" />
        <arg line="-storetype" />
        <arg line="pkcs12" />
        <arg line="-keystore" />
        <arg line="${certificate.ios.cert.file.path}" />
        <arg line="-storepass" />
        <arg line="${certificate.ios.password}" />
        <arg line="-provisioning-profile" />
        <arg line="${certificate.ios.provisioning.file.path}" />
        <arg line="${project.publish.path}${file.separator}${ios.app.file}" />
        <arg line="${ios.app.descriptor}" />
        <arg line="${project.build.path}${file.separator}${project.output.swf}" />
        <arg line="${ios.app.icon.path}iOSicon-29.png" />
        <arg line="${ios.app.icon.path}iOSicon-57.png" />
        <arg line="${ios.app.icon.path}iOSicon-512.png" />
        <arg line="${ios.app.icon.path}Default.png" />
    </java>
    <eclipse.refreshLocal resource="${project.name}" depth="infinite" />
</target>
```

And since this target depends on the air.compile-to-air, a SWF file will be made first. That SWF will be cross-compiled to a native iOS *.ipa* file with ADT. With this (and the help of ADT), you can create an iOS app on all operating systems that Ant runs on! Very cool, right?

Let's see if you can create your own targets to make your app ready for the App Store.

You can, of course, extend these build files with targets that create the device-specific *app.xml* for you, so you don't have to create them manually. Create once; save time later.

If you want to test your iOS app, you can just drag the *.ipa* file to iTunes and sync it to your phone. Voilà! You have just created your first iOS app with Ant! Congratulations.

Other Cool Stuff to Do with Ant

There are tons of other cool things you can do with Ant! You are only limited by your imagination. Have a look though the Ant manual and see whether there are other tasks that you could use in your daily workflow, because not all the examples provided in this book might be the right fit for you.

If you want to notify yourself of a completed build while away from your desk, for example, you can use Ant's Get task to hook into a script that sends you an SMS message. (Yes, I do. And I use Twillo, an SMS provider, for it. It has a really good and simple API for this.)

You could also tweet your build result with Ant's Get task. Or post to a website, or maybe even your company's intranet. For this, you would again use the Get task. (The Get task also supports authentication!)

Or you could combine all the knowledge you've gained from this book and build a project creator that takes user input and writes a complete project—even the property and build files, filled in with the correct properties—based on template files. The possibilities are endless!

It doesn't matter what you think of, the most important thing is that you *make it work for you*. If you know Java, you can also extend Ant with your own tasks. The online Ant manual provides you with good documentation to get you started.

Happy coding!

About the Author

Sidney de Koning is a full time geek. When he was 8, he got hooked on BASIC on his grandfather's Amiga 500. Now he still gets excited developing mobile applications and websites. His passion is to play with technologies like Adobe's AIR and the Android platform, and he loves to translate complex abstract ideas into concrete usable applications.

He started programming in Turbo Pascal and Delphi, and tried PHP, but later found his true love—Flash. Now Sidney is a Flash Platform developer with more than 10 years of experience in ActionScript (1, 2, and 3), AIR, and lately also Android. And a little iOS.

After setting up the online department at the Dutch MTV in 2005, he freelanced and worked for smaller companies until 2009. He has worked for and with a multitude of companies including MTV, TMF, Nickelodeon, Media Catalyst, and Code d'Azur. His current employment is at LBi Lost Boys in Amsterdam, where he develops in AS3, solves technical problems, and acts as technical lead. His specialties are streamlining development processes, AIR, and AIR for Android. In his spare time, he has written content for the Dutch Adobe User Group and taught programming classes at the international SAE College.

From writing articles on blogs to writing magazines and a book, and from teaching students programming to coding and talking about code, it all has to do with transferring knowledge and inspiring people who share the same passion: creation.

He likes to keep sane by meditating, reading, writing, and running. He also maintains a weblog about AIR, mobile, and Flash development at *http://www.funky-monkey.nl*.

Get even more for your money.

Join the O'Reilly Community, and register the O'Reilly books you own. It's free, and you'll get:

- $4.99 ebook upgrade offer
- 40% upgrade offer on O'Reilly print books
- Membership discounts on books and events
- Free lifetime updates to ebooks and videos
- Multiple ebook formats, DRM FREE
- Participation in the O'Reilly community
- Newsletters
- Account management
- 100% Satisfaction Guarantee

Signing up is easy:

1. **Go to: oreilly.com/go/register**
2. **Create an O'Reilly login.**
3. **Provide your address.**
4. **Register your books.**

Note: English-language books only

To order books online:
oreilly.com/store

For questions about products or an order:
orders@oreilly.com

To sign up to get topic-specific email announcements and/or news about upcoming books, conferences, special offers, and new technologies:
elists@oreilly.com

For technical questions about book content:
booktech@oreilly.com

To submit new book proposals to our editors:
proposals@oreilly.com

O'Reilly books are available in multiple DRM-free ebook formats. For more information:
oreilly.com/ebooks

O'REILLY®

Spreading the knowledge of innovators   oreilly.com

The information you need, when and where you need it.

With Safari Books Online, you can:

Access the contents of thousands of technology and business books

- Quickly search over 7000 books and certification guides
- Download whole books or chapters in PDF format, at no extra cost, to print or read on the go
- Copy and paste code
- Save up to 35% on O'Reilly print books
- **New!** Access mobile-friendly books directly from cell phones and mobile devices

Stay up-to-date on emerging topics before the books are published

- Get on-demand access to evolving manuscripts.
- Interact directly with authors of upcoming books

Explore thousands of hours of video on technology and design topics

- Learn from expert video tutorials
- Watch and replay recorded conference sessions

Spreading the knowledge of innovators   safari.oreilly.com

Lightning Source UK Ltd.
Milton Keynes UK
UKHW030609260719
346817UK00005B/533/P